ALL THE GARDEN'S A STAGE

Choosing the Best Performing Plants
for a Sustainable Garden

JANE C. GATES

With illustrations by the author

Schiffer Publishing Ltd)

4880 Lower Valley Road • Atglen, PA • 19310

Other Schiffer Books on Related Subjects:
Petscaping: Training and Landscaping with Your Pet in Mind, 978-0-7643-3854-0, $24.99
Creating Curb Appeal, 978-0-7643-3278-4, $24,99
Hardscaping with Decorative Concrete, 0-7643-2598-1, $19.95

Designed by *Danielle D. Farmer*
Cover Design by *Bruce M. Waters*
Type set in Bernhard Tango Swash/Latin Bold Cg/NewBskvll BT/Helvetica Neue LT Pro

ISBN: 978-0-7643-3979-0
Printed in China

Schiffer Books are available at special discounts for bulk purchases for sales promotions or premiums. Special editions, including personalized covers, corporate imprints, and excerpts can be created in large quantities for special needs. For more information contact the publisher:

Published by Schiffer Publishing Ltd.
4880 Lower Valley Road
Atglen, PA 19310
Phone: (610) 593-1777; Fax: (610) 593-2002
E-mail: Info@schifferbooks.com

For the largest selection of fine reference books on this and related subjects,
please visit our website at **www.schifferbooks.com**

We are always looking for people to write books on new and related subjects. If you have an idea for a book,
please contact us at **proposals@schifferbooks.com**

This book may be purchased from the publisher.
Include $5.00 for shipping.
Please try your bookstore first.
You may write for a free catalog.

In Europe, Schiffer books are distributed by
Bushwood Books
6 Marksbury Ave.
Kew Gardens
Surrey TW9 4JF England
Phone: 44 (0) 20 8392 8585; Fax: 44 (0) 20 8392 9876
E-mail: info@bushwoodbooks.co.uk
Website: www.bushwoodbooks.co.uk

GATES THEATRE

A Schiffer Publishing Co. Production

To Barbara

My helpful sister, toughest critic, and very best friend

Acknowledgments

I extend special thanks to all the people who helped me and supported me while I floundered about putting this book together. I am grateful for those who put up with my neglect and short temper when I felt stressed and those who encouraged me when I wasn't sure which way to go. I am thankful for those of you who plowed through the many drafts of this book and offered advice, corrections, and valuable suggestions. Shirley Bovshow, Frank Stetson, Yolanda Vanveen, Sue Meeks, Karen Geller-Shinn, Wilma Arste, and Maryam Hamedaninia: your input has been invaluable.

All the wonderful photographs from so many different locations were possible only because of the contributing photographers in this book. Many thanks to Diane Sullivan, Velvet Heller, Kylee Baumle, Teresa Soule, Lisa Bourey, R. Lutz, Mark Holland, Genevieve Schmidt, Mary Kirtland, Katie Elzer-Peters, Robert Bornstein, Jane Milliman, Jenny Peterson, Barb Black, GardenSoft, John at Easy Living Wildflowers, Ray at Forest Farm, and Laura and Paul at Wildflower Farm.

Additional thanks goes to the public and private gardens and nurseries where I found material for this book to photograph: Annie's Annuals & Perennials, Richmond, California; Castaic Water Agency—Conservatory Garden and Learning Center, Santa Clarita, California; CSUN Botanic Garden, Los Angeles, California; Ganna Walska Lotusland, Montecito, California; Green Arrow Nursery and Garden Center, North Hills, California; Green Thumb Garden Center, Santa Clarita, California; Hannah Carter Japanese Garden, Los Angeles, California; The Japanese Garden at the Tillman Reclamation Plant, Van Nuys, California; Mildred E. Mathias Botanical Garden at UCLA, California; Santa Barbara Botanic Garden, Santa Barbara, California; and Theodore Payne Foundation for Wildflowers and Native Plants, Sun Valley, California.

This book would never have been completed without the content, photographic expertise, and personal support given by my dear friend Velvet Heller, and my sister, Barbara Black. I never knew there was so much involved in writing a book and I am very grateful for the gift of these two people in my life. Thank you, both.

One last thank you goes to the editors and staff at Schiffer Books who made this book possible.

CONTENTS

All the Garden's a Stage
Choosing the Best Performing Plants for a Sustainable Garden

I became a fan of Jane Gates' writing and landscape design expertise through reading her garden column for Examiner.com as well as her blog, "GardenGates.info." Jane caught my attention with her beautiful garden designs and, even more impressively, with her creative spin on the most mundane subjects such as landscape drainage, grading, and irrigation. Not sexy subjects, but indispensable information for constructing viable landscapes.

An original thinker, Jane Gates won me over.

Little did I know how deep Jane's fountain of inspiration ran! I later discovered that along with garden design, Jane was a multitasking, multitalented artist, accomplished in painting, drawing, illustrating, cartooning, and even music writing! Jane was also plotting to write a book.

Here it is!

When I read Jane's manuscript for this book, it struck me how clever the analogy was to equate garden plant selection as an "audition" for a garden show. This is a subject I know something about! I'm a garden designer in Los Angeles, a garden television host (*Discovery's Garden Police*), and garden show producer for the web, "Garden World Report." I've been to and conducted many auditions for shows and I've designed close to one hundred gardens.

It's a great analogy!

Consider the similarity: there are millions of people who would sell their soul to be selected for a television show and there are just as many plants that can be considered for a coveted spot in your garden! Although plants don't have a soul to sell, they have roots that long to be established in fertile ground where they can perform as promised in garden books such as this one. (Make sure to read the Chapter 6: "Plant Character Profiles").

On the one hand, there are countless plants to "audition" for your garden, but not every plant that catches your eye is suitable for the role it must play in your garden. For example, Jane breaks down specific "roles" that plants undertake based on your "micro-climate."

"Moisture Mavens" are plants that thrive in rainy climates and don't mind humidity. The opposite, "Denizens of the Dry," as Jane refers to them, are the camels of the garden world, content with a spritz of water now and then. "Beach Babes," on the other hand, are plants that crave the salty air, sandy soil, and plentiful sun.

By giving plants memorable names based on common characteristics, Jane personifies how they are similar to human beings. I fancy myself a succulent plant as I'm happiest in warm, sunny weather and I am, by nature, a low maintenance person.

What kind of plant are you?

All the Garden's a Stage is written for the beginner gardener as well as for the person accustomed to having dirt under their nails who may desire more learning. The book gives you a primer on the essentials required to keep your plants alive, introduces you to a cast of memorable plant characters, and takes you through maintenance and design. It's all here, so take the book for a spin and get ready to produce an award-winning garden show in your own yard!

Shirley Bovshow
Garden Designer and Garden TV Producer
GardenWorldReport.com

Introduction

🌱 your garden show

People love plants and plants certainly can benefit from people. Whether or not plants are capable of loving people is still somewhat in doubt, but there have been some really interesting research tests — done by humans, of course — that have measured the electronic responses from plants in response to human moods. Whatever the emotional connection between plants and people may be, it is clear that growing plants indoors and out is a favorite human pastime that seems to work well for both humans and plant life alike.

Still, there are a lot of people who claim to have no luck growing plants. Chances are if you've had trouble, it has little or nothing at all to do with love, your mood around plants, or any belief that you don't have a green thumb. In fact, all wise plants know that there are only a limited number of reasons people have trouble making plants happy. You can pretty much guarantee if you are struggling to make your plants thrive in your home or in your garden it's due to one of three basic issues.

1. BASIC PLANT NEEDS:

All life on this planet shares the same fundamental requirements for survival. Plants don't always have the same needs that people do. Although we humans expect plants to fit wherever they look best, sometimes where they look best is not going to give a plant what it needs to perform well. We need to understand the basics for good plant growth.

2. WHAT DIFFERENT KINDS OF PLANTS NEED:

Often people think they are treating a plant right when, in fact, a lack of knowledge about the individual plant's profile can lead to mistakes in care.

3. MAINTENANCE:

It is simply human nature to become busy and forget to give plants the extra help they need when they are growing in the unnatural environments that people have set up for them. Plants can't yell when they need attention. If you want to be successful, it's best to set up systems that will help give each plant what it needs most — just in case you become too busy to remember.

Growing a successful garden is really just a question of getting to know your plants and getting comfortable with providing the things that will help them grow well. To make a decorative landscape you will need a lot of ornamental plants to work together both aesthetically (to create a total picture) and practically (to help each other thrive). Yes, indeed, plants will interact and have either a positive or negative effect on each other. To make your garden grow to be both beautiful and healthy, you will need a varied cast of horticultural players that support each other to create the show you want in the climate and soil of your garden.

Plants evolve naturally in different climates with different soils. Each adapts to its own native environment. As a result some plants respond better to a lot of sun while others insist on more shade.

Some thrive in heat that will stifle others. Soils can be wet or dry, sand or clay, sweet or sour, sodic (high sodium or salty), or not. Some plants bask in plenty of humidity while others have adapted to desiccating winds. There are even plants that perch on rocks or tree branches and don't expect soil to tickle their toes to allow them to grow.

Plants work together in a garden in myriad ways. Apart from choosing plants that need similar conditions to share the growing area, there are other interactions that impact plant growth. Sometimes plants help each other in more obvious ways like offering shade for each other or providing support for their climbing buddies. There are also the more subtle interactions that have a powerful impact on plant growth. Some plants exude chemicals that discourage others from growing too close.

There is also a fine fungal network, known as the mycrohizza, which interconnects the root systems of all plants in their natural environment. Although people can't see this living network, it's hard at work all the time, carrying moisture and telegraphing messages about stresses and neighborhood changes from plant to plant. This fungal network is different for each micro-environment and is a vital asset to the survival of each living colony of plant life. Even though this is a relatively recent discovery for human scientists, plants have been part of this network for the millennia.

Don't worry, though; you don't have to become a scientist to grow a healthy, happy, and lovely garden. If you set up your garden with the basics and choose the right profiled plants to give them what they need, Mother Nature is likely to choreograph the show and you won't even need to know about all the details.

If you want to grow a garden filled with show-stopping, happy plants, you need to become familiar with the climate and conditions in your landscape. By realizing that your garden is a whole, interconnected network of interdependent pieces on which life depends, you can create your own successful garden version of a Broadway play by making sure you set the stage properly. However, you need to understand the cast of plant characters you plan to use in your landscape so you audition and choose the right players.

setting up the audition

Auditioning your plants before buying them will allow you to select cast members that will not only create the drama you want in your garden, but will perform their roles naturally and show off well. Choosing the right plants will make maintenance a lot easier for you. You can mix different plants with different needs and ignore the stage on which they are performing, but it will be a constant battle to try to keep each plant happy.

There are so many combinations of conditions across the planet. It's impossible to cover all the different environments where plants can grow. Yet the majority of plants are quite adaptable and, if the essentials are offered, plants from similar conditions can often be grown in different gardens in foreign landscapes across the world.

The good news is that this offers an ever-widening selection of plant choices for your garden. It also offers opportunities for plant breeders to cultivate exciting new varieties to introduce into the horticultural market. On the downside, sometimes these new players are so happy in their new quarters that they take over and become invasive pests. Examples are the Spanish brooms or the pampas grasses that have been imported into Southern California, the water hyacinths that are clogging some Florida waterways, or the Japanese honeysuckle that has invaded countrysides and woodlands all across the United States. These guys have become so happy in their new homes that they've bolted outside their gardens and are bullying out some of the important native plants that offer homes and food to local wildlife, upsetting the balance of that interdependent natural network of life. So always check with your local Department of Agriculture if you think there might be a chance you are planting an imported pest into your garden. Nobody likes a stage hog.

Become familiar with the cast of plants from around the world and the varied conditions in which they grow. You don't have to know all the possibilities. Just check out your favorite plants and see if they will be compatible with the conditions in your garden. Or research plants from different parts of the planet that grow in conditions similar to those in your landscape to see how many possibilities there are for your own garden. One way to have fun while checking out potential plants is to visit some of the small, lesser-known, local, public, private, and university gardens. Unlike the larger gardens, these are more likely to be designed to fit into a more limited, natural ecology.

Sometimes you can alter your soil or add more shade to accommodate a plant you like. Most plants have a fair amount of flexibility. However, the further you stray from a plant's ideal conditions, the more of an effort it will be for you to maintain unnatural conditions in your garden to keep your exotic addition healthy and happy. Be realistic about how much work you are willing to do before committing yourself to the constant labor of supporting one special plant.

Although this may all sound like an awful lot of knowledge to put together, it really isn't as demanding as it may seem. If you become familiar with the workings of nature's overall gardening plan and then understand the environment you have on your own property, it becomes a lot easier to know what character plants to cast into the roles you want for a beautiful yet easy-maintenance garden. It really is like putting together your own show. Again, you don't have to memorize all the different plants and what they require, you just need to check up on the plants that catch your eye and make sure they are a good match for the role you want them to play in your garden performance.

That said, it's worth taking a peek at some of the major environments on planet Earth where so many of the potential plant players for garden landscaping have evolved. This will introduce you to the cast of horticultural characters from which most of our garden plants have been bred. After all, who better to let you know what plants really want and how to give it to them than the plants themselves?

Plants are at home in
places all over the earth.

Section One

Schiffer Publishing

Ready to Write a Book?

We're always seeking authors for a wide variety of topics. This is your opportunity to shine! See our website to view an extensive list of our titles. If this idea appeals to you, we'd love to hear from you. Review our book submission guidelines at our website by clicking on the "Submit a Book Proposal" link. Then email your proposal and ideas to **proposals@schifferbooks.com** or write to the attention of **Acquisitions** at the address below. You can also call 610-593-1777 to make an appointment to speak with an editor.

⊗ Schiffer Publishing
has books covering a wide
variety of interests including:

Antiques, Collectibles, & The Arts
Advertising • Automobilia • Black Collectibles • Breweriana • Ceramics • Clocks • Corkscrews • Decoys • Dolls • Fine Art • Folk Art • Furniture • Graphic Art • Holidays • Hunting • Jewelry • Kitchen • Lighting • Leatherwork • Metalware • Native American Crafts • Nautical • Pinball • Quilts • Rugs • Sports • Teddy Bears • Telephones • Textiles • Toys • Video Games • Vintage Fashion • Watches • Writing Instruments and more.

Design, Lifestyle, & D-I-Y
Architecture • Astrology • Counter Culture • Culinary Arts • Erotica • Interior Design • Kitchens and Baths • Landscaping • Numerology • Paranormal • Pin-Ups • Pop Art • Tarot • Tattooing • Textile Design • UFOs • Witchcraft • Basketry • Beads & Jewelry Making • Carving • Furniture Making • Gourds • Home & Garden • Metalwork • Modeling • Pyrography • Sculpture • Textiles • Weaving • Wood Turning • Tools and more.

Military, Aviation, & Automotive History
WWI & WWII Armor/Aviation: German • U.S. • British • Russian • the Jet Age • Unit Biographies and Autobiographies • Edged Weapons • Firearms • Uniforms and more.

Maritime
Seamanship • Navigation • Ship Management • Towing • Transportation • Boats & Boat Building • Medical • Legal and more.

Regional
History • Children's Books • Architecture • Photography • Landscaping • Paranormal • Souvenir • Guidebooks • Cooking and more.

To learn more, go to **www.schifferbooks.com**
Call 610-593-1777, 8:30a.m.-5:30 p.m. EST
or write to 4880 Lower Valley Road
Atglen, PA 19310 USA
and ask for a free catalog(s).

In the UK and Europe contact
Bushwood Books at 44 (0) 20 8392-8585
info@bushwoodbooks.co.uk

PLANT GROWTH FOR DIFFERENT CHARACTER ROLES

Basic Plant Needs

The first issue to address for a successful garden is to know what different kinds of plants need to thrive. Plants, like people, depend on their environment for survival. They are not humans, they are not pets, nor are they inanimate objects. Plants are living creatures that evolved on the planet the same as other forms of life. Although there are some plants that have adapted to some pretty astonishing environments and can live with virtually no water, or underwater, in low oxygen elevations or despite high mineral concentrations in soil, all plants are living things and need the same basic elements of life. Look at the elements of water, light, air, food, and temperature in your garden and audition the kinds of plants that will give you the look you want while growing best in the conditions you can supply.

If you were to cast different characters for a play, you would look first at their physical attributes. Chances are you will look for someone eye-catching for the lead role...just like you will want a showy plant for your garden focal point. You might want a strong group of singers for a back-up chorus or some sympathetic characters for supporting roles. The plants you choose for your garden need to act together to create a total work of art. Profiling your plants will be a bit different than auditioning actors or singers. You will want to mix different growth habits, foliage forms, colors, textures, and flowering times to create an on-going, living show. To do this you need to keep in mind the basic structural differences in plant growth.

There are certain characteristics all plants share. Before you can even hope to hold auditions, you need to understand the basics of what your performers will need. Leaving behind much of the theatrical analogy, these next sections are focused on providing information to help you understand the raw materials that provide motivation for your cast of plants to grow in your garden.

All plants essentially grow from tiny beginnings that encapsulate all the essential genetic material to form a mature plant; seeds and spores (the latter for simpler plant life like ferns or mosses). Just like an egg, seeds will grow if given the proper environment. Adding water, light, air, and the right temperature will cause germination and the miniscule spark of life will use whatever food it finds to begin to grow. Different plants grow in a variety of ways, but most start with one or two leaves, grow stems, spread leaves, and eventually flower. Green plants make food and grow by photosynthesizing water and nutrients from the soil and air with light by using chlorophyll in their leaves and stems. Some will grow large like trees and develop woody stems that will harden into trunks. There are those that will stay soft and pliable and twine or clamber their way up other vertical surfaces in the form of vines. Yet others will grow into clumps or fashion food storage roots that will become bulbs, corms, or tuberous roots. Then there are those that will spread wide, stretch tall and thin, or bloat stems or leaves into water storage tanks like many cactus or succulent plants. All, then, will bloom in their own, special ways.

People often choose plants for their garden simply because of the flamboyant displays certain flowers, leaves, or even stems or bark can give. Flowering can take place with single blooms, clusters, or sprays. Some blooms are insignificant and the foliage creates the visual allure. There are multiple groups of blooms, often grouped in ornamental arrangements, that tend to be less colorful but interesting in shape and form like the inflorescences most grasses produce. There are many oddities like the fig tree that actually blooms thousands of tiny flowers hidden inside the fruit rather than on the outside where flowers are usually seen.

No matter how a plant flowers, it will need to be fertilized to produce seed for the next generation. The majority of plants have stamens that produce pollen grains (male parts) and pistils (female parts) that, once fertilized by the pollen, will swell at the base of the faded bloom to create a fruiting capsule containing the seed(s). Many plants grow these male and female parts both contained in an individual flower that is called a 'perfect flower' or *hermaphrodite*. There are also plants that flower only with either male or female flowers called *dioecious* that need to be planted near each other if you want pollination to take place. There are even plants that carry separate male and female flowers on the same plant, termed *monoecious*. However the job gets done, the goal is that the pollen that contains the male sperm makes contact with the female pistil to create the seed. The capsules in which seeds develop are sometimes even more ornamental than the flowers and these plants are grown for their colorful or sculptural pods, berries, or other seed containers. Many berries and fruits are edible and create the basis for much of the food mankind depends upon for sustenance.

Because plants will adapt their habit of growth to the surrounding environment, you will find all sizes, shapes, and textures of leaves, bark, flowers, and fruit. Not only will these habits of growth offer you a variety

Sharp and thorny plants make good guards. Use them to discourage unwanted animals or under windows for security.

of physical characteristics you can use to design your garden show, but they can offer clues to the character of the plant and help you cast that plant in the right role for your garden. For example, if you come across a spiny plant, you can probably figure that this plant has learned to wear armor to protect itself from munching critters that would be likely to devour it for dinner if it were unprotected. If you have a garden where hungry wildlife is a problem, this bristly-clad fellow might be just the perfect choice to cast for the role of sentinel along a fence line or out in the open.

Blending the habits of growth aesthetically into your landscape is one element you may want to use in designing your garden show. You can also use the different flowering and fruiting times of your selected plants to orchestrate blooming throughout the growing season. As different groups of plants fade, others can reach their peak like a succession of new acts in your garden play. Keeping in mind how your plants grow will also help you choose plants that will re-seed where you want them

and avoid plants that might become genuine nuisances where you don't want them. Apart from looking at the physical adaptations of different plants in your garden, you will want to blend them with the environment of your personal living space so you can easily supply your plants with what they need to thrive. (We will get into orchestrating and directing your garden show a little later.)

You will be sharing your garden habitat with your chosen plants and since all living things have many needs in common, you may find growing plants isn't as unrelated as you might expect. Just like human beings, plants need water, light, air, food, and reasonable temperatures to survive. Because the members of the plant kingdom process these elements differently than people and because they can't just get up and move to improve conditions, their needs are a bit more exacting.

WATER

The first thing people need to keep in mind is that all life on this planet needs water to survive. Just because a plant has adapted to a low-water environment like a desert cactus or a chaparral scrub plant does not mean that plants can live without water.

Though there are rare exceptions — like the resurrection plant (*Anastatica hierochuntica*) that can live without water for years as it blows around its North African desert home curled into a dormant ball, nurturing a small amount of moisture in its center — sooner or later it needs to come out of dormancy and grow again — and that means it needs water. When the rains finally arrive, the resurrection plant unfurls, turns green, and enjoys the wet weather...until things dry up and it goes into near-death dormancy once again. Okay, there is a bit of a myth to this story because the real truth is that the plant is an annual and actually does die. It harbors seeds inside that germinate with the first moisture so the plant appears to resurrect. However, even the resurrection plant needs water to produce its miraculous growth.

Whether dry-adapted or not, you can figure out how much water your chosen plants are likely to need by looking at where the plant originally developed. Meeting a plant's basic water needs is essential to helping it grow happily. If you grow plants in containers, they are yet another step removed from a natural environment and containers are likely to dry out faster than the open earth. Containers also have a very limited depth, so roots cannot reach down for lower water tables as they would do if they were growing in the ground. Nope, no getting too far away from water! Even the best low-water adapted growing things need to get a drink to keep their tissues healthy.

Over-watering can be just as damaging as under-watering. Unless you are growing a plant that has evolved to cope with a very wet environment, too much water can squeeze out air pockets from soil. Most plants need that air to help their roots breathe so if it gets sodden, the little root hairs that take up water with the help of air cannot function. They rot and die and even though the plant is actually drowning, it might wilt and look like it needs more water because it is unable to drink up the water it needs from the water-logged roots. This is where it is good to profile your plants so you know what kind of watering each kind of plant needs to thrive.

The Resurrection Plant.

Then there is the quality of the water itself to consider. Like soil pH, plants can be affected by the pH (the measurement of acidity versus alkalinity) of water. Although often much of your tap water comes from local sources that are likely to echo the pH of your local soil, occasionally your tap water may be quite different from the soil in your garden. Sometimes the pH of the water you use can mediate the soil you are watering and sometimes it can concentrate problems. Water quality, content, and pH can vary widely. Neutral pH is not acid or alkaline and has a value of 7. Although the pH scale ranges from 0 to 14, most plants do best in acid or 'sour' soil between 5 and 7 or alkaline or 'sweet' soil between 7 and 8.5 with increments of one-tenth of a percent at a time.

A garden of acid-loving plants will thrive in sour soil.
Photo by Genevieve Schmidt.

Acid soil lovers tend to grow on soils with a lot of organic materials that break down to create sweet soils. Soils with higher quantities of dissolved minerals — and often less organic matter — tend to register higher than the neutral pH of 7. The higher pH numbers are home to base or alkaline-loving plants. Examples of acid-lovers would be heather, blueberry, azalea, camellia, pine, and fern. Examples of plants that thrive on alkaline soil would be the lilac, clematis, Echinacea, lavender, poppy, and rosemary. The majority of edibles in the vegetable garden tend to prefer soil and water slightly on the acid side.

In addition to pH, there are other nutrients, minerals, and chemicals that can be found in different waters. There are waters that are perfectly natural yet can be heavy in salt, arsenic, copper, or many other elements that can prove toxic to plants, people, or animals. Plants all over the world have adapted to areas with different concentrations of varied materials. Some need these chemicals or minerals in their water or soil to thrive. If you want to grow some of these specially adapted plants, knowing their profiles will help you figure out what they need to perform at their best.

Water from the tap is often high in fluoride and other protective chemicals added by people for human health and safety reasons. Many of these additives will dissipate when left in open air (but not all). If you are growing sensitive plants, like many types of tropical plants or orchids, you might want allow your tap water to sit in an open container for an hour or so before watering them to lighten the chemical burden.

Most recently many cities have been changing over their disinfectant water treatment from chlorine to using chloramines. Whether or not this is a good thing is still being debated. It is important to be aware that chloramines do not dissipate in standing water anywhere as quickly as chlorine, so it will not help to age your water (unless you wait for a week or two) to remove it. Chloramines will burn fish, amphibians, and invertebrates so be very careful when adding tap water to water gardens with fish or other living creatures. The chloramines in ordinary tap water can quickly kill your fish if they are not sufficiently diluted or filtered. Plant growth seems to be unaffected, but there are still concerns being voiced about the possibility of build up in the soil. There is no quick or easy solution for removing chloramines other than putting your water through a filtration system should the chemical worry you. So far, even sensitive plants like orchids seem to have shown no adverse effects.

Basic Plant Needs

LIGHT

Another necessity for plants to grow is light. Some plants are adapted to lower lighting than others. Some grow under the cover of heavy forests or between sheltering rocks and can tolerate appreciable shade in the garden or even the low light of residential houses and commercial environments. If you forget how little light there is inside a home, just try taking a photo without a flash and see how dark your pictures look. Human eyes can adjust to different light levels, but plants create food with photosynthesis. They can only do so with the nutrients available from soil and air mixing with water and put into action with light from the sun. The light may not have to be direct sunshine, but it has to be enough to allow a plant to process these basics if it is going to live. Low light might make a plant struggle to live: too little light will kill it.

One telltale characteristic of too little light is a pale, thin, and distorted look to new growth. Sometimes new shoots will become elongated as they stretch for light. This kind of growth is called etiolation. If you see your plants sending up new growth like this, they are telling you they desperately need more light.

Not only is it necessary for plants to get sufficient light, but those plants that evolved in shade can burn to a crisp if you set them out to grow in blazing hot sun. In fact, even a natural sun-lover that has been kept in low light for a period of time can burn if moved into full sun too fast. If you move a plant outdoors after it has spent the winter snuggling inside your low-light house or you buy a plant that has been displayed in the shade for some time, it should be slowly acclimated to full light so it has time to adjust.

This cactus grew in full light, then in too much dark (notice how it shrank and became etiolated) then filled out again once returned to good light. *Photo by Velvet Heller.*

FOOD

Like all living things, plants need food, too. Plants extract their vitamins, minerals, and trace elements from their food source by using water. Of course, very few plants go hunting like animals for their food, but there are some that actually do. Well, sort of. These are known as carnivorous plants and some are quite fascinating in their habits of growth. As a result, it's not uncommon for some people to grow these insectivorous plants indoors or in outdoor gardens where conditions can support them. The sundew, Venus flytrap, or one of the various pitcher plants like the *Darlingtonia Californica* are examples of plants that lure insects into traps so they can digest them in exuded acids and process the nutrients into plant food. It's curious that some people are uncomfortable with the concept of carnivorous plants when these plants are not all that different from a human luring in a fish with bait.

Most plants have a more simple process for gathering food. Nutrients are harvested from the air and soil. The most common way plants get their food is to leach it from the soil and drink it up through the roots with the help of water. This is why most

Carnivorous plants like the pitcher plant invite insects in for dinner.

plants get into trouble if under-watered since they can't get a necessary, food-rich drink if the soil is too dry. Equally, over-watered soil or soil with poor drainage can drown root systems. So too much and too little water can both keep a plant from getting the food it needs to thrive.

There is a very close relationship between soil and water that offers food and enables plants to feed. Both water and soil vary widely in acidity, organic materials, and mineral content. Knowing your own soil and water can be a major consideration in profiling your plants successfully. Different plants have evolved in soils with acid or alkaline soil; some are comfortable in well-drained soil, whereas others like moisture to collect around their roots. Plants have evolved in clay, peaty, sandy, salty, stony, soggy, and many other types of soil. Matching your own soil with those of the plants you are auditioning for your garden show can make the difference between getting the performance you want — or not.

There are kits you can buy to test your soil make-up. You can also have your soil tested by your local agricultural department to get in-depth information. You can easily figure out which of the basic three categories your soil is by yourself; they are sand, clay, and loam. Squeeze a handful of slightly wet soil in your fist. If it crumbles apart readily, chances are you have sandy soil. Soil that clings together in a tight ball reflecting the impression of your hand is probably high in clay. A handful that loosely retains its shape is either a combination of clay and sand or is likely to be a good loam. There are plants that prefer different kinds of soil so one type of soil is not necessarily better than another.

Plants that grow in the ground are considered terrestrial. There are also plants that have adapted themselves to growing above the soil. These plants are called epiphytes and tend to grow on tree limbs, rocks, or other places rather than in the ground. These guys use their roots more for stability than for feeding. Plants like some of those in the *bromeliad* family can adapt leaves into special vases for catching mist, dew, and rainfall.

Other epiphytes extract water and minerals from the air in the form of humidity, rainfall, or condensation with their open leaves or specially

Epiphytic plants like some orchids, bromeliads, or this insectivorous pitcher plant will perch in the air. *Photo by Diane Sullivan.*

adapted aerial roots. Epiphytic orchids like Vandas or Phaleanopsis are typical examples of these plants. You can grow epiphytic plants in pots with large slits or holes cut in them to offer plenty of air circulation around the roots. Don't use soil for most of these plants, but instead pot them up with bark pieces that will allow for air circulation around the roots and fast water drainage. Water accumulating around the roots will suffocate the roots and kill the plant. Different epiphytic plants grow with different needs, so the right care will depend on the type of plant.

There are also plants that are parasites or partial parasites. Not many people grow parasitic plants in their homes and gardens — at least not intentionally.

A common semi-parasitic plant in warm climates is the mistletoe. (It does have some chlorophyll so it creates some of its own food, but it siphons most of its energy off its host tree.) Ah, yes, many people think this decorative little plant that dangles romance during the Christmas holiday time is something charming, but for trees that have been infested with big growths of mistletoe, the roots that penetrate into the cambium layers of host trees can eventually kill off large limbs. If the parasitic plant feeds too heavily off of its host tree or plant, it can eventually kill it. Be aware, however, that nature doesn't just create bad guys without redemption. The trees may not benefit much from these energy-stealers, but the birds seem to grow healthy and strong in areas where they can feed on the mistletoe berries. There are only a small number of decorative parasitic or semi-parasitic plants that are grown in gardens or greenhouses as curiosities: most are considered to be undesirable in the garden.

AIR

Plants, just like people, need to breathe. They cannot grow without air. Although some water plants have adapted to getting oxygen and nitrogen out of water so they can grow submerged, most plants breathe through pores in their leaves and need good clean air to thrive. If you let your houseplants get too dusty and dirty, the pores (stomata) will get clogged and it will be difficult for the plant to breathe, much like it would be for a human being to having airways restricted. Gardens where there is a lot of wind, dust, or road traffic can also suffer from breathing difficulties, especially if there isn't regular rain to wash them off. Areas with heavy air pollution can stifle healthy plant growth. You might even notice leaves looking burnt in climates where there have been excessively hot or dry winds. Most plants breathe better with higher humidity and leaves can parch in very dry air. Occasional overhead irrigation can also help clean leaves. If you live in a normally dry or windy climate, choose plants with profiles that have the character you need to handle the demands of your environment.

As you get to know the different accommodations that plants make to thrive in the natural environment where they evolved, you will see that many of the different leaf forms have taken shape to adapt to air, light, and humidity. Keep in mind the wide range of decorative formations when you audition the plants you want in your garden. Sometimes these practical habits of growth will suggest design ideas to you. Other times the leaf forms will be clues to help you know where to best plant the selections you buy.

As you audition these plants for your garden show, that performance is as important as beauty. A plant that hails from the hot, dry bushland of Australia

Plants breathe with stomata that open and close like microscopic little mouths.

is likely to be happier in the inland California or Texas chaparral garden than a closer relative from the cooler, moister shoreline of California or Texas. Even if you like the flower of that coastal dwelling plant better than a more adapted plant, over time your poorly adapted choice will likely languish and look far less beautiful than the happier chaparral choice.

People often talk about how it is healthy to have house plants in the home because photosynthesis allows the plant to take in carbon dioxide and give off oxygen. Human lungs thrive with more oxygen than carbon dioxide — in fact, one of the many elements involved in air pollution is the higher percentage of carbon dioxide released into the air due to burning fossil fuels and industrial processing waste. Too much carbon dioxide can be dangerous, even lethal, to human lungs. So, when plants filter out the CO_2 and add oxygen to the air, it is indeed helpful to the human body.

However, people also should be aware that when the sun goes down, plants stop photosynthesis because they no longer have the necessary ingredient of sunlight. This will mean the extra oxygen put into the air as a by-product of photosynthesis will discontinue. Plants breathe both day and night, and that action does release small amounts of CO_2 into the air. Since the overwhelming addition of oxygen takes a snooze for the night while breathing continues, this is where the belief that plants 'pollute' the air with CO_2 at night comes from. Plants release no more CO_2 at night than they do during the day: they simply stop offering the bonus of extra oxygen. Of course, most house plants do not make much of an impact on indoor air quality either day or night since they make up such a small percentage of interior functional space. So don't go setting your plants on dollies to wheel them in and out of the house daily.

Plants need air in the soil as well as aboveground. The air around their roots allows them to suck up food dissolved in water. This is why it is not advisable to walk around or dig your plants in the garden right after watering or after a measurable rainfall. In addition to the muddy mess you'll create on your feet, you will be compressing the soil and squeezing out those essential air pockets. It is also why it can be difficult to grow plants on land that has been unnaturally compacted, like after heavy construction machinery has been in the area.

TEMPERATURE

Nature has created remarkable diversity in plants. The plant kingdom has adapted to most climates on this planet in one way or another. Apart from water, light, food, and air, plants need to handle the temperature range in which they will grow. If you want your plants to be happy and healthy, choose varieties that can adapt to your local temperature range.

Curiously enough, if a plant has a chance to get habituated to a new home, it is likely to withstand temperatures that may sneak outside of the usual comfort zone. The most critical time is the first year or two when new arrivals need to establish a good root system and adapt to their new surroundings. It is not uncommon for recent arrivals of the same plant variety to freeze during a cold spell while their established kin brave the frosty weather without any

Native plants can thrive even in extremely cold climates like here near Antarctica in Punta Arenas, Chile. *Photo by Diane Sullivan.*

setback whatsoever. Hot sun can burn easily, too. Just because a variety of cactus is comfortable in its desert home doesn't mean the same type of cactus raised and coddled in a comfy human greenhouse won't fry into a toasty brown if suddenly exposed to roasting sun.

Some plants evolved in cold areas, some in warm. Some handle wide temperature ranges while others don't like a lot of variety. Look at the freezing point

Basic Plant Needs

as a critical borderline. Some plants can handle no frost at all and will melt into a pile of brown mush should the temperature drop below freezing for even an hour. Most tropical plants will survive a couple bouts to freezing, but others will fade away if temperatures flirt anywhere near that point-of-no-return very often. A lot of plants will take varying degrees of cold under freezing. Going dormant in the cold is a common adaptation plants have made to deal with frosty temperatures. Some are fine so long as there is no 'hard' frost where the ground itself freezes solid. These plants won't tolerate having their roots freeze and are best dug up for the winter. Other plants absolutely demand their icy cold winter breaks so they can reset their internal clocks and charge into healthy growth in the spring. Without their winter snooze these plants simply decide life isn't worth living. Once again, check into the profile of the plants you want to grow. Make sure they are comfortable with the temperature ranges in your garden. If you are determined to import a prima donna plant into a leading role in your landscape, remember you will have to give that plant special treatment. That will mean you'd better plan on investing a little more time and energy to give it the special care it needs to protect it from harm.

One thing plants will really appreciate is a chance to become used to their new surroundings. Since many plants are raised far from where they will eventually make their permanent homes or in radically controlled environments like greenhouses, they can find your garden a bit of a shock. If you haven't bought plants from a local grower or garden center where you know the plants have had some time to adapt to similar air, water, and light conditions, you might want to allow your new arrivals an opportunity to get used to their new surroundings before plunking them into the ground. By letting a newly purchased member of your garden sit for at least a day or two in the location where it will be planted, you will be giving it a chance to adapt somewhat to the new spot before it is subjected to the further stress of planting. Do make sure the pot doesn't dry out during this 'hardening off' time, however. Potted plants can dry quickly especially in warm or dry weather.

Temperature ranges impact plant growth from two different sources. There are the effects of air temperature and the effects of soil temperature. Delicate plants can often brave colder air so long as their roots remain snug and warm. Frost can drift down on cold air currents, so sometimes you can over-winter a frost-shy plant in cooler temperatures than you'd expect so long as you give it overhead protection to keep frost from settling on the leaves. Only the more cold-tolerant plants will handle soil that freezes hard. Keeping soil warmer than air is one of the benefits of mulching plants. Wetter soil also tends to stay warmer than dry soil. Since water will freeze at 32 degrees Fahrenheit (0 degrees Centigrade), moist soil will tend to hold longer at the freezing point whereas dry soil can quickly drop in temperature to match the air.

Air, temperature, and water can also blur the lines a bit in the form of humidity. You might have noticed that some plants can take a wider variation of temperatures when there is more or less humidity. Looking at this process simplistically, plants pull up moisture and food through their roots and breathe out excess oxygen, carbon dioxide, and moisture through those pores (stomata) in a dance called transpiration. High humidity with little air motion means the released molecules breathed out will just hang around near the leaves. (It is this surrounding moisture that freezes and paints a coating of ice crystals around plants when you see frost on your outdoor plants in winter.) There are plants that need a lot of

Tropical plants in Cairns, Australia put on an exotic show in a warm, moist environment. *Photo by Diane Sullivan.*

more vulnerable to temperature changes if it isn't all plumped out with plenty of water.

Give your new arrivals a little extra TLC. If you live where sun is bright or hot, a little extra shading will be welcomed. If the weather is chilly, sometimes you can offer a little extra warmth by placing a stone or a block of cement nearby to absorb daylight sun and release a little radiated warmth at night. Or try offering a little overhead protection. And I repeat: leaving new arrivals in their pots in the locations where they will be growing for a few days before planting usually gives them a chance to acclimate to their new homes better.

Once you feel comfortable with the general needs of plants, you will be able to take a little tour of your own garden space and pay attention to what you have already there. Once you are familiar with your property's environment, you will know which areas will offer different water, light, food, air, and temperature conditions.

summary:

Casting Call

Now it's time to get back to auditioning these plants for the garden. All this basic information on plant growth should make you a better director and help define not only what plants look best, but which will perform the way the script of your garden demands. Use the water, light, food, temperature, and humidity information as cheat notes as you look through the hopefuls lined up to audition for your garden.

It will be much easier to maintain a successful landscape comprised of well-matched performers than to try to change the major conditions of your environment to support inappropriate plant choices just because you like the way a plant looks. You may have to compromise and pick a less glamorous leading lady in favor of one that is better adapted to your local conditions, but a happy plant will end up looking better than an unhappy one (especially if the unhappy one dies). A cast of garden growers that perform well together will make your overall design into a rave performance. You don't need one temperamental star to destroy your whole garden show.

moisture in the air. This high-humidity environment is common to heat-loving plants that have evolved in places like the tropical rainforest.

Drier air and faster moving air currents will suck away the released moisture and work vaguely like a vacuum making the plant suck up more moisture from the roots. Plants accustomed to dry or windy native homes do well with faster transpiration. Most tend toward woody stems and smaller leaves that don't need to store as much water as the humidity-lovers. These guys are going to sulk if you add humidity to the cold temperatures they might ordinarily tolerate.

In short, humidity can effect how a plant reacts to surrounding temperatures. A dry-adapted plant is more likely to rot with too much humidity just as it will with being watered too much. A humidity-lover is

Bringing the Characters Together

CHAPTER 2

A happy cast of plants form a colorful bouquet in the garden.

This garden has happy performers that like the script they follow. Plants that are well adapted to their role look their best and are easy to maintain. Photo taken at Annie's Annuals & Perennials, Richmond, California.

CLIMATES, SPECIAL ADAPTATIONS, AND CROSSOVERS

To grow a garden successfully, you need to know what your plants expect. Since every plant has adapted to the native conditions where it evolved to get the light, food, air, temperatures, and water that are basic to all life, knowing a little about those conditions will give you clues as to which plants will audition best for the environment in your own garden. First you can think about how your plants will look together as a community. Then take a look at what kind of plants you want for your cast. Do you need water mavens? Is your garden space better for mountaineers? Or perhaps you need to cast some of the denizens of the dry to create the best performance in your landscape climate.

Many gardens offer different conditions within the same space. These conditions define the roles you need your plants to play. Good drama actors rarely do well in comedic roles. The better job of casting, the better performance you are likely to get — and this will translate into saving you time and money in maintenance, too. You can mix different

Lupines have adapted to diverse climates. These are growing by the roadside in southern Chile. *Photo by Diane Sullivan.*

This is the *Lupinus nana* at home in the dry desert or chaparral.

Yet another species of Lupine finds a home in the mountains of Isafjord, Iceland. *Photo by Diane Sullivan.*

plants with different needs, but it will be a constant battle to try to keep each plant happy.

Climate, special adaptations, and crossovers are some categories that will help group some basic plant needs by environment. In Chapter 6, there is a sample list of selected plants if you want to read up on more detailed individual plant suggestions.

Different climates can have a combination of temperature, humidity, and exposure effects that may vary over altering topography, sometimes changing within short distances. These are usually referred to as micro-climates. There are landscapes that can have different micro-climates within a single property. For example, the summit of an exposed hillside might sustain different plants from the base where there will be different wind effects, shade patterns, and where cold might settle differently. You may find that a plant that does well in one part of your property does not like another.

There are also plenty of plants that are willing to share the stage with plants from other categories.

A selection of water mavens can make their homes in the tropics or the forests. Dry denizens are found in deserts, popping up in the prairies, or hanging out in high mountain elevations. There are country cousins perfectly happy to pal around with woodland plants, or even snuggle up to some of their favorite beach babes. There are even plants that have developed species in a wide range of diverse climates. The lupine, for example, has adapted to different locations all over the world producing such a wide range of species and cultivars that there is probably one that's right for almost any landscape. Just make sure the variety of lupine you choose for your garden is one that will like your garden conditions.

Use these categories as guidelines, and check the resumes of whichever plants you are interested in auditioning for your garden show. If your own garden is a close match to one of these profiles, you will have an easy time identifying which plants are going to like living in your landscape and which ones are not.

Ponds are complete, contained environments.

MOISTURE MAVENS
The bog, pond, and river nymphs

The surface of the planet earth is covered by more water than land, and Mother Nature has seen fit to adapt plant life to live in these moist environments. For the gardener, this means that wetter areas of the garden will be a perfect home for these masters of moisture. Some homeowners own property that comes with naturally built-in streams, ponds, bog areas, or other wetlands. Other people build ponds, streams, and other water features into their landscape for the soothing sound of water and the reflective beauty of refracted light. As we become savvier about our water use, landscapers and garden designers are learning to design water features for drainage, cleaning, and filtering excess water as it is reintroduced back into the groundwater. These moist areas can create ideal habitats and watering sites for native fauna, especially important where building has encroached on local wildlife habitats. They create the perfect spot for growing the moisture-loving plants that have evolved naturally in wet conditions. Having a moist area in the landscape is the only way you can plan on growing some of these lovely and occasionally odd-looking water-lovers.

Moisture mavens are plants that are experts of coping with a wet environment. Like all general habitat profiles there are wide variations in the preferences of different water-loving plants. There are moisture-lovers that like to grow in a garden with damp soil, those that like their toes wiggling in water, while others need to be swimming up to their necks. There are even plants that need to float on the surface of water. Some of these plants need sun and some need shade, but all moist-growers have the commonality that they will not tolerate having their roots dry out. Some larger, thirsty plants have roots that penetrate deeply to chase moisture down into the ground allowing them to handle more surface dry. Bog plants, on the other hand, usually need the security of being in contact with water constantly.

Water-adapted characters come in all sizes and shapes. There are trees that grow by rivers and streams like willows and birches. These are stream-side growers and can wander some distance from running or standing water. Moisture spreads out below ground from lakes, rivers, and streams. These trees will need to grow where there is a high water table or plenty of rain to flourish. Although you can plant them in drier areas, they are likely to lack the robust health necessary for them to fend off disease and insect attacks when deprived of the copious water they crave. There are individual plants that are highly tolerant of diverse conditions and will grow both in water and in the regular garden. The decorative Louisiana hybrid iris and the canna lily are examples of these flexible growers: both grow with specially adapted storage roots called rhizomes that probably afford them more tolerance to different moisture conditions. Not all plants with rhizomes do well in these varied conditions, however.

Bog plants are fond of dipping their toes in water. Some will hang out in mud or wet sand and others are happy with water pulled up snugly to their leafy arms. If you want to grow these plants in pots rather than directly in the ground — as in most specially constructed water features — make sure you plant them in a heavy clay soil that will not wash away easily. Since bog plants do not need drainage like most other plants, drainage holes in their pots are not necessary. In fact, any hole larger than a quarter inch is likely to invite the soil inside to slither away into surrounding water, making a mess at the bottom of the water feature and leaving

This pond has a variety of water mavens that enjoy different growing conditions.

no anchor for the plant's roots. So opt for pots without holes for plants needing submerged containers.

The penultimate water mavens are the swimmers. These plants cruise happily on the surface of the water; some with underwater roots hooked into cracks, crevasses, or nestled into soil at the bottom or side of a body of water. A few enjoy floating free, their roots dangling just beneath the water surface. Although often these plants seem to sport smooth, sturdy, dry leaves, if you remove them from their aquatic environment even for a short time, they will shrivel up into a dried crisp due to their high internal moisture content.

Fish often like to feed on the roots of floating plants so plan carefully when raising fish and floating plants in the same environment. Tiny plants are nourishing for hungry fish and large koi love to root around at the base of planted water lilies, often uprooting the plants. Decide how you want your plants to interact in your garden environment. Choose the appropriate species of both plant and fish to create a self-supporting ecosystem where destruction may be factored into the design. You can also protect specially planted areas with added materials like stone and netting. On the whole, fish and plants do well together. The plants help oxygenate the water and shade the fish from hot sun whereas the fish waste offers food to the growing plants. In the water environment, the living cast members all have to get on well together.

For the most part, pond plants will grow and bloom best if they get at least six hours of sunshine during the day. Green plants are less demanding of sunshine. In general, water-loving plants can tolerate drier or variable conditions with added shade. Learn the needs of each individual water maven you want to add to your garden. The best plant to win the audition for your showy, wet garden is the one that sports the look you want while fitting into the environmental conditions of your space. If you have any really wet areas in your soil or you have open water that needs planting, water mavens are the ones to invite to your casting call.

The woodland and water plant communities meet together in this New England landscape painted by Mother Nature. *Photo by Barbara Black.*

FOREST DWELLERS
Lovers of the shady woodlands

Plants that dwell in the forest or woodlands have evolved in their own special world. Trees cast a lot of shade and rain down leaves — a few at a time if they are evergreens, or in an annual downpour if they are deciduous. Plants tend to grow together and spaces fill in with ground-cover, lichens, and mosses. Forest dwellers are used to a fair amount of rainfall that allows them to grow in a community with plenty of water to share. The combination of rain and the moisture created by the transpiration (breathing) of all those living leaves adds more humidity to the air. As a result the climate in a woodland ecology is usually moist, somewhat humid, and offers plenty of shade. The moisture encourages the constant supply of fallen leaves and old growth to break down into compost. Older forested areas can have deep layers of compost that has built up over hundreds of years and supports much of the woodland growth. The action of rotting material then adds an element of acidity to the soil. You can pretty much expect most plants that have evolved in these conditions to prefer moist, shady or semi-shady, and slightly humid conditions with soil rich in organics. It is also likely your favorite forest dwellers will prefer a soil that is more acid than alkaline. Most of the woodland inhabitants will be used to at least some protection from direct, heavy winds, too.

Not all forests are alike and there are plenty of environmental variations. There are dryer woodland areas and boggy spots. There are wooded areas in colder parts of the world that spend long winters snoozing under blankets of ice and snow, and warm, wet forests of jungles or swamps. Some forests reach up to high elevations, quitting only when they reach the timber line, whereas others have created specialized homelands, with dotted plants unique to extreme conditions like the Joshua Tree Forest in the California desert. When auditioning roles for the forest dwellers, make sure your garden offers the setting of a similar wooded area. If your garden offers matching conditions, you will probably have an easy time growing forest dwellers. For purposes of this book, we are looking mainly at the more commonly pictured forested regions of the temperate climates rather than the specialized, adapted areas.

Woodland plants vary in the amount of shade they need. In higher elevations, lower rainfall, or rocky substrata, growth is likely to be sparser and there will probably be more sun penetrating to the ground. Soils will also vary. For example plants that grow under fir trees tend to enjoy a more acidic soil. The soil pH under conifers is likely to be on the acid side so expect rhododendrons, ferns, azaleas, and berries (like blueberries) happily taking up residency. These plants prefer a rich soil with plenty of compost. Plants that naturally grow under the

The woodlands have given birth to many showy garden plants. Here are ferns unfolding in the forest. *Photo by Barbara Black.*

canopy of trees are going to be subject to a continual litter of organic material — leaves, pine needles, spent blooms, seeds, etc. Humidity is likely to be higher with the canopy holding in moisture. Forests tend to grow thickly where there is no shortage of rain or underground moisture.

For the most part, think of your forest dwellers as plant types that don't mind occasionally rubbing shoulders with each other. Think of them as the kind that will enjoy the shade cast from tree tops like the shade from an umbrella. They seem to be more secure with that sense of closeness and protection. They're social fellows that like to work together in their woodland environment to keep each other company. These are characteristics you can look for when auditioning these performers for a forest or woodland setting.

Give your woodland plants good drainage. They are used to soil that is filled with organic material and plenty of tiny air pockets so water drains away. You may find the occasional water-mavens that will hang around streams, ponds, and lakes in the woodlands, but for the most part, your plants will enjoy rich, moist soil that drains well. There are forest dwellers that will not mind periods of sunshine or dappled shade. There are those that will prefer to hunker down into pockets of deeper shade. Almost all will like growing rich and green since they don't have to deal with desiccating sun or winds.

If you want to grow woodland plants in pots, keep the same conditions in mind. Give them a soil with plenty of organic matter that drains well. Compost often works well mixed with garden loam, and then set them where they will get gentle sun, part shade, or full shade, according to the needs of the individual plant. Make sure your pots never dry out too much.

If you are growing your garden near natural woodland areas, chances are your home was once part of the forest, too, and your soil will be ideal for forest plants if you plant the right plant in the right exposure. As always, using local natives will be the easiest and best match for your woodland garden.

MOUNTAINEERS
Residents of the highlands

Often called alpine plants, these residents of the higher elevations are fond of cooler temperatures and firm footing that drains water quickly. Our planet offers a fascinating assortment of natural stage settings. One of the more challenging environments is where the mountaineers spend their time. Plants that grow in the higher elevations of the planet's crust are usually hardy fellows.

Although their terrain and weather conditions can vary widely, a number of mountaineers can be found hanging out in sparsely wooded areas or high up where the air is thin and there is little protection from whatever the weather decides to deliver. Some in the lower mountain elevations offer highly adaptable garden plants that can fit into the regular garden border while those from higher altitudes — often referred to as 'alpine plants' — have adapted to handle everything from thin soil to harsh temperatures and sun exposure above the timber line. Few of these highland plants grow to lofty heights as the soil is likely to be rocky, fast-draining, and winds are often intense.

There is a wide range of mountain-growers that have acclimated themselves to thrive in heat and cold, rain and dry, snow and sun. The ultraviolet rays are strong at these higher altitudes and may be responsible for the often bright colors found in alpine flowers. Flowering is timed for the best possible conditions, so most mountaineers bloom neither very early nor very late in the season. To grow well no matter what nature throws at them, these hardy alpine plants usually keep a low profile, frequently in spreading mats or snuggling clumps.

If you want to plant these higher elevation residents in your garden — and you don't live on the face of a cliff or a mountaintop — you can keep them happiest by building them rock gardens. Some mountaineers have very specific requirements that will make them tough to grow in the home garden, but there are a surprising number of alpine plants that are willing to adapt so long as you give them excellent drainage. Of course, that explains the idea behind a 'rock' garden, since adding plenty of rock will help the soil drain quickly as well as adding the rocky feel that looks right with the habit of growth seen in these mountaineers. Rocks and stones also help mediate the air and soil temperature because they are so dense that it takes them a long time to

both heat up and cool down. This storage of cold and heat helps to reduce the fast-changing temperatures of high altitude air.

Another characteristic of a lot of alpine plants is their preference for sweet (alkaline) soils. This is a logical adaptation for plants that evolved in exposed, rocky areas where the soil is comprised of eroding mineral rock than layered organic matter. The alpine plants that prefer a soil with a higher acidic content are those that grow in high forests or near streams where rotting material has been able to collect over time to create a richer, moister humus.

If you live in a higher elevation environment, these mountain plants will be colorful and low maintenance performers in your garden. Don't be put off by the sparse growth of these native plants. With a good design, they can be planted close together and create a stunning effect.

For most lower elevation gardens, lots of these mountaineers will find a happy spot in your garden if they have their preferred conditions. There are plenty of ground cover plants in this category that will tumble over walls, spill out of pots, fill in hard to grow areas, and handle those difficult hillsides where they will get their good drainage while making a welcome artistic statement in your garden design. Don't bother auditioning tropical beauties or beach babes for a rocky, high elevation garden. They will be totally miscast. Instead, go for the mountaineers. These guys have the motivation and the talent to deliver what you need for a great performance.

DENIZENS OF THE DRY
Plants that have adapted to dry air, hot summers, and low rainfall

There are places in the world where rain does not fall regularly. Leafy inhabitants need to adapt to the lean soils that are often filled more with minerals than the organic remains of previous growth. With lower rainfall there is usually low humidity and plenty of strong sunshine. Plants that evolved in places like the desert or chaparral have made special provisions to adapt to these conditions. Occasionally they've also had to adapt to wide daily temperature ranges.

If these plants could talk, they would tell you that they can take a lot of weather extremes so long as you make sure you give them really good drainage. Good drainage means that no matter how hard it rains, water will not sit around their roots for long. Although, like the mountaineers, the denizens of dry areas demand fast drainage, these plants are quite happy living in lower altitude geographic areas, often inland, with very low humidity. Thriving in this lack of humidity (along with a resistance to bright, hot sun) is one of their special talents. Whereas the forest dwellers are used to growing closely with shared humidity, water, and shade, the denizens of the dry spread further apart to claim whatever moisture they can. They have learned to handle unrelenting sunshine with their hard, waxy, or coated leaves, and to conserve their energy in semi-dormancy at the hottest time of the year so they can burst forth with a brilliant show when the conditions are just right.

There are tough plants in this category that have adapted to long, parched conditions by storing moisture in leaves or modified trunks making them succulents. (Note that although there are numerous cacti and succulents that grow in arid environments, all cacti and succulents are not denizens of the dry!) The denizens of the dry frequently adjust to waterless seasons by looking forlorn during hot summer months as they go through a semi-dormant period. They rest up to resume active growth when the rainy season begins. Still others simply have short growth seasons so they can take advantage of the best weather conditions.

Another characteristic found in many arid plants is a fine, delicate, leaf construction. Whereas tropical plants tend to have broad, large leaves that collect rain and the moisture from high humidity, the finely cut foliage allows for reduced transpiration and a reduced profile

Bringing the Characters Together

for blustery winds. Transpiration is pretty much the way leaves breathe and it involves losing more moisture for those with bigger and broader leaves. Other adaptations to heat and dry can come in the form of lighter, grayer foliage, fine hairs that create a fuzzy texture, a slower and tougher growth habit, or even the ability to shrivel up sufficiently to revive in better conditions.

Surprisingly, there are dry-adapted plants that bloom with very showy flowers. These are more than welcome in the decorative garden — even in areas that may not demand drought-resistant types. If you want to grow them in your landscape successfully, you need to give them the essential conditions that mimic where they evolved. Give them sand, gravel, or other fast-draining materials in their soil. Hillsides drain faster than flat lands, but high humidity will make growing these plants difficult. Don't situate them near water features or boggy places, and only a few will do well in shade. Warning: If you give these plants too much water, rich soil, or feed them generously, many will grow lush and fast, making you think you've helped them grow successfully. Giving them conditions that are too kind will force soft, over-blown growth that will overtax their systems and destroy them in no time, cutting their life spans very short. They may look great, but they won't survive being spoiled for very long.

However, if your script calls for a tough, drought-resistant cast of characters, call the agents (garden centers) that represent the denizens of the dry. You might be surprised at the wide range of looks and personalities available in these plants.

The denizens of the dry have evolved habits of growth that let them take advantage of dry air, fast drainage, and low rainfall.

Even dry-adapted native gardens can look lush and colorful.

TROPICAL BEAUTIES
*Plants that come from warm, humid homelands
that offer generous rainfall*

The tropical beauties have evolved in high humidity climates with plenty of water and gentle temperatures. Large, glamorous leaves that collect moisture from frequent rains, mists, or thick fogs are a common growth adaptation. Leaves can have a rich green coloring. In these moist, tropical jungles some plants don't even need to grow in the soil. With sufficient moisture in the air, there are those that have decided to dance in the trees, balance on a limb, or snuggle into a rock crevice adapting roots as much to hold onto their perches as to filter out food from the moisture around them. The tropics are home to some of the most flamboyant-looking leaves and flowers since these lucky plants are living under their own ideal greenhouse system.

Unlike plants adapted to harsh conditions and hungry soils, these plants grow where centuries of heavy growth has laid down a thick layer upon layer of rich humus as plants die and rot back into the soil leaving behind their organic content. Plants from warm, steamy climates are used to plenty of moisture around their roots. They don't have to worry much about cold temperatures or dry winds to tatter big, broad foliage. They can flower during much of the year since they don't have to hide from inhospitable winters. Give your tropical plants similar conditions if you want them to remain true beauties.

Many people are enamored by the huge flowers, interesting forms, brilliant colors, large ornamental leaves, and lush growth typical of most tropical growers. These plants will adapt to gardens in warm climates if you can give them the humidity and rich soil they expect. Cooler or drier climates will require special efforts to keep them healthy. Very few of these lush plants can handle frost. Some flinch if the temperature slips under 50 degrees Fahrenheit. The most fragile will need to be grown in greenhouses or in terrariums, but like so many performers in the plant world, many of the tropical beauties have proven themselves more adaptable than you might expect. Understanding what your plants need to thrive may be enough for you to give carefully chosen delicate-growers a home in your non-tropical garden — with a little extra effort.

You'll also find a number of plants in this category that will tolerate light to deep shade. The rampant growth of tropical jungles sometimes doesn't allow much light to penetrate through to the plants below. Some of these plants show up in garden centers as ideal houseplants. Others are willing to make small compromises in similar environments like parts of Florida, coastal Southern California, and other warm climates as well as gentle-weather regions outside of the United States mainland.

When growing the tropical beauties in containers, give them a rich, loamy soil, good light, and *don't* let them dry out. Humidity is important and hard to maintain in the interior of the average home, so set the containers on trays filled with pebbles and then add water so it does not touch the bottom of the pot. Air must enter the drainage holes under the pot and the pebbles should support any container above the water line. The rocks will also help break up the surface of the water adding more surface area to evaporate into the air around your plant, creating a mini-environment of higher humidity.

If you can provide a warm, moist environment for your plants, you can enjoy some of these highly showy plants in your garden, home, office, or greenhouse. As with all plants, there is a wide range of conditions that fall under any one category, so some will be easier to grow in your particular environment than others. The tropical beauties like being pampered. They often come painted with colorful makeup and costumed in lush foliage. Use these glamour girls only where you can provide them the stage setting they demand.

Bringing the Characters Together

PLAINS POPULATION
*Inhabitants of the central areas of North America
and at home in the prairies*

When we think of the vast area that stretches down from Canada into the south of Texas, east of the Rockies, and in the middle of the North American continent, we are reminded of the large, open expanse that has been cultivated for years and has been known as the 'bread basket' of America. This area is the native home to many ornamental grasses. These roaming plains mostly cover an area about five hundred miles wide and sit at between 2,000 and 5,000 feet in elevation. A large percentage of these plains are considered the Great Plains and are coated with a deep layer of rich soil deposited by the ancient glaciers. There are some smaller areas on the slopes and in bog areas where rains are heavier and soils drain slower, but much of these prairie lands receive less than twenty inches a year. Torrential downpours are common, but so are times of drought.

In the shadow of the tall Rockies, trees are less abundant in the prairies. There is little erosion when compared to most other topographies of the world. Over history the area has been heavily grazed by bison, deer, and elk. As a result, trees are scattered singly or in small stands and so it is a characteristic of the Great Plains that there are no heavily forested areas. Instead, deep-rooted grasses have colonized the rich soil; their penetrating roots make these plants able to handle droughts as well as rain and most of these grasses enjoy the open sunshine or light shade found throughout the prairies. You can see why this area has become the 'breadbasket' of the country. It was historically a major grain-producing arena for wildlife, but over the last few centuries, with its rich soil and efficient drainage, it has been readily taken over by farming. It is the birthplace of many of the ornamental grasses — some hybridized to make them even showier — that are gaining so much popularity in today's landscape designs. This is where you may be most likely to find the right players if you have ornamental grass roles to be filled in your garden.

Mixed in with grasses are other native plants that enjoy the same conditions. Plenty of the flowering plants are colorful and will adapt well to the home garden. If the conditions in your garden are not too different from those of the Great Plains, you might want to consider auditioning some of the performers from the plains population to grace your landscape. Due to their need for good drainage you might find some of the plains population amenable to joining denizens of the dry, some beach babes, and even some mountaineers in sharing space in a well thought out garden design.

The plains are home to some popular garden plants like this field of *Echinacea simulata*. *Photo courtesy of Easy Living Wildflowers.*

Line up some of these residents of the plains for an all-American contingent in your garden show; these are the original 'home on the range' cast members, equally at ease moseying across the steppe, grassland, or hanging out in the prairie.

BEACH BABES
Plants that love sunbathing on the coast, scantily clothed in only leaves and flowers

Beaches come in an assortment of environmental conditions. There are ocean shorelines that lap up into the sandy beaches where people love to tan themselves on beach towels, but there are also rocky ocean shorelines and beaches around inland, saline, or freshwater areas that can be boggy or filled with sedge meadows. There are even areas where forests creep up to waterlines or spill into the tangle of heated swamps. There are thousands of miles of coastal property around the world that outline all the dry land raised above the oceans. The coastline residents are plants that are adapted to well-drained, sometimes sandy soils and can tolerate salt spray. Salt can be lethal to many plants so it takes a really well-adapted sunbather to thrive in beach conditions. Coastal weather is impacted by onshore and offshore winds, humidity, fog, and the other effects resulting from the proximity of large bodies of water.

Most shorelines have adapted to the regular invasion of water and the effects of any deposits left from past incursions of tides and currents. As a result, the home for the majority of plant root systems is usually one of fast-draining sand, stone, or rock. Although there are exceptions, most areas of beach do not have tall or heavy growth. The lack of a heavy canopy of tree branches means that the majority of beach dwellers love to hang out in the sunshine whenever it is not diminished by fog or cloud. Being near plenty of water, beach babes usually enjoy a fair amount of humidity and are accustomed to wearing the occasional beaded moisture of fog. Unless the beach babes grew up in inlets or freshwater shores with high water tables — many of these would fall under the category of water mavens — these plants expect to have fast-draining soil. As growing areas move further inland, richer soil is likely to mix with the sand or rock, giving way to a wider range of plant life.

Air temperatures near oceans, seas, and lakes are mitigated from the wider ranges further inland. It takes a long time to appreciably change the temperature of a big quantity of water, so large bodies of water will keep temperatures less extreme on the coast than the land-locked areas.

If you live near a lot of water, invite the beach babes to your cast party: they'll love to play in your garden. If you want to grow any of these plants in pots, mix a little sand or gravel into their potting soil to help with drainage and make root conditions a little more like home. Some of these plants do well in other climatic conditions despite having proven themselves resilient to beach conditions.

COUNTRY COUSINS
The reliable, adaptable garden plants that blend into many garden scenarios

The country cousins include the population of most of our common garden flowers. The open countryside is home to plants of all descriptions. There are country cousins native or cultivated all over the world. They happily reside in fields and vales and perch on gentle hillsides or in stands of close growth. Some tiptoe into boggy areas or settle into dry spaces, but most of these plants are at home in rich soils with plenty of gentle sunshine and a fair offering of annual rainfall. There are country bumpkins and country gentlemen. Some accommodate themselves to cold, snowy winters while others enjoy mild weather year-round. Audition some of these country cousins for a wide cross-section of scenarios. They can adapt to surprising extremes and cozy up to mountaineers, water mavens, and dry denizens in high or low altitudes in the less extreme home garden.

Plants in this category are not adapted to high drama, demanding environments. They will brave the occasional incursion of nasty weather, but for the most part are not expected to cope with difficult soils or radical temperature changes. Those that live in cold-winter climates often sleep quietly through the worst of the weather and happily yawn back into growth when springtime wakes them up. There are some that are an exception to the rule, but even they will enjoy the comfortable conditions of the average garden.

Some of the plants I am categorizing as 'country cousins' are plants that are considered 'old fashioned'. Most parts of the United States were settled by England, France, and Spain. These historical settlers brought with them their favorite and familiar garden plants. Perhaps the largest influence in gardening has come from the United Kingdom. Traditional gardens are still created with a number of plants that were common to the cottage garden or formal English garden for centuries. A lot of these plants are being bred for new and interesting cultivars, but even the old varieties still hold their allure. Since these gardens were developed in a climate that suffered few extremes and experienced plenty of natural rainfall year-round, the country cousins have settled in well as general garden plants in many different types of landscapes.

On the whole, country cousins grow well with average soil and average watering. These plants originated in places all over the world, but became high demand garden performers internationally due to their versatility. The majority are well-known, but just because they are famous does not mean they'll be pricey. Quite the opposite: due to high demand and the good job of hybridizing agents, lots of country cousins have become celebrities that are affordable in almost any garden show.

SUCCULENTS AND CACTI

Sometimes a plant's adaptation is not characteristic of only one area. For example, areas that may be warm or cold, high or low, or have rich or hungry soils may also go through periods of drought. To store water over these periods, some varieties of plant life have adapted stems, roots, or leaves to swell with water and carry life through dry times. These are most commonly seen in the form of cacti and succulents.

Succulents

Of all the different kinds of plants, there is no group with more variety in size, shape, color, and texture than succulents. Succulents are plants that have adapted to their environment by evolving the ability to store water in altered leaves or stems. By storing water in the plant tissues, these plants can handle uneven rainfall and the occasional drought.

However, because succulent adaptations have occurred in a variety of climates, not all succulents will thrive in the same conditions. There are succulents that can take the cold and those that are frost sensitive. Some bask happily in full sun while others demand shade. Certain species can take dry soil whereas others need more water. Just as different plants grow in different conditions, succulents also take an assortment of forms from tall to short, fuzzy to smooth, rosette (leaves forming in a circular pattern like an unfurling rose) or sword shaped. Because there is such a wide range of growth habits in the world of succulents, they offer many different plant effects you can use for designing.

Succulents can be designed with other plants to offer texture and sculptural forms. They can cover ground where other plants will suffer from overly fast drainage. You can use their variety of texture and color to create whole gardens of their own. They are ideal for planting vertical walls or green roofs where their small roots and spreading habits can be fashioned into patterns or pictures.

Succulents are simply plants that have adapted their leaves and stems to hold extra water, which tides them over during dry spells. This ability to store water has evolved because most of these plants live in climates where either they cannot grow elaborate root systems or where periods of drought are common. The majority are at least somewhat drought-tolerant. Succulents can tolerate a surprisingly large amount of water so long as the water drains off quickly. Standing water around roots is sure to kill them. The most common causes of cactus death in the garden are because of shriveling from very little water or rotting from wet. The best rule of (green) thumb for cacti in general is to keep them dry in cool or cold weather.

Cacti

Due to their capacity to store water, some succulents have formed into bizarre shapes and forms. Many have decoratively shaped and colored leaves, and some have very showy flowers. All cactus plants are succulents; however, not all succulents are cacti. Cactus plants are defined by having spine cushions called *areoles*, usually in a somewhat evenly spaced pattern. New growth can start from any of these areoles. There are succulents that have spines, but they do not grow out of these circular spots. Areoles will produce not only the spines of a cactus, but the flowers, fruit, and offsets or new vegetative growth. If it doesn't have areoles, then it isn't a cactus!

The same water-storing ability that helps most succulent plants to survive dry air and erratic water availability makes those that developed in warm climates vulnerable to freezes. The water they store in the cells of those swollen leaf or stem adaptations can turn to ice and burst the living cells. Cactus and succulent plants that evolved in colder climates tend to evolve thicker cell walls. Grow only the succulents that are comfortable in cold climates if you live in a frosty area. Although a lot of succulents can handle hot sun, some need more shade. Most all cactus and succulent plants do well with light colored gravel or sand mulch that will drain quickly and show off their interesting growth habits.

Plant succulents close to the soil surface so only the roots are underground. Planting them too deeply will likely cause them to rot. Unlike other garden plants most succulents do better planted dry, encouraging

Some people might think this *Agave americana* variety is a cactus. It lacks areoles, so although it is a succulent, it isn't a cactus.

No aeroles here either. Both of these are only succulents: a *Stapelia* and probably a *Sedum*.

RIGHT: You can see the evenly spaced aeroles on this Opuntia cactus plant.

Cactus and succulent gardens can be designed into a dramatic landscape. Photo taken at the Dadd-Griffith Residence.

the roots to reach out for moisture: new plants are best if they are not watered in. Some will even grow roots easily from broken pieces and will form colonies around the mother plant from rooted leaves or snapped stems.

Cactus and succulent plants are performers with unique talents to deal with water availability. There are those that bloom with amazingly showy flowers and those that offer sculptural growth habits or leaf forms. These performers can work as actors, props, and even take part in the architectural set design of your landscape.

BULBS, CORMS, TUBERS, AND RHIZOMES

This is another adaptation in which plants from all kinds of climates have chosen to build their own storage compartments. Because of this clever little trick, bulbs, rhizomes, corms, and tubers are in high demand for roles in the garden audition department. These plants come in neat little dormant packages that make them easy to ship, sell, and plant. Many of these plants offer showy flowers, decorative foliage, and can be very easy cast members to work with. Often passed over by landscapers who need the garden to look impressive when they finish installing it — and dormant bulbs look like nothing short of a patch of blank soil when first planted — bulbs, rhizomes, corms, and tubers can give a garden some of the flashiest flower shows. They tend to be short-lived, so add them to your landscape like glitter or fireworks to brighten up the performance every now and then.

These plants are remarkable adaptations. Nature was really clever when she decided to pack up some of her plants into little packages complete with everything they need to grow. With these little life-containers neatly tucked away, plants can slip back into a dormancy that will keep them safe and sleepy while growth is inhospitable. Then, when conditions become favorable, everything has been conveniently stored right there to get things growing again. In short, we're talking about garden performers who come fully costumed with everything they need to put on their show. Yet there is a difference in the storage set-ups between bulbs, corms, tubers, and rhizomes.

A bulb garden in full bloom in Holland. *Photo by Mark Holland.*

BULBS

Bulbs are interesting because essentially they are miniature baby plants enclosed in a layered format. Picture an undeveloped bud with the beginnings of a stem and surrounded by layers of leaves all condensed into a small package — sometimes even encased in a papery wrapping. Familiar bulbs would be tulips, daffodils, hyacinths, and the familiar onion.

Bulbs contain the whole plant like an egg.

CORMS

Corms may look a lot like bulbs, but they function differently. These are adapted root systems that contain food for the plants, but do not encase immature leaves or flowers. Think of them as solid little containers filled with the nourishment the plant will need until roots can form and take over as the contents of the corm is used up. Always leave leaves to die back naturally after the plant blooms so the energy can drain back down to the roots to form new corms for the next year's growth. Common examples of corms are lilies, Crocosmias, and gladiolus.

Corms are storehouses.

TUBERS

Tubers are usually rather lumpy-looking, living containers that are a compact, compressed food source studded with 'eyes', or growth points, from which plant leaves and stems will grow. The potato is a typical tuber, but so are dahlias, Anemones, and Ranunculus.

Tubers are inflated storage roots.

RHIZOMES

Rhizomes are actually adapted swollen stems rather than roots. They often have a long, bumpy habit of growth, more like a swollen branch or a fingered hand. All rhizomes bud and grow from this storage stem that lays on or under the ground like a bulb or tuber. You might recognize the rhizome in the form of a fresh ginger root, the bearded Iris, or the canna lily.

Rhizomes are inflated stems.

INVASIVE PLANTS

Although this book is intended to help you define what different garden plants need so you can match them with the conditions of your garden, there are some plants that can do too well.

There are some good reasons to audition only local native plants. As I mentioned before, these plants offer the homes and food sources to local wildlife that imported plants usually do not. Local natives are easy to grow since you know your soil and air will be a perfect match. Once established, these plants will require only the maintenance necessary to keep them neat within the landscape design you have created. Since native plants are growing in leaps and bounds in popularity, plant breeders are creating showy hybrids and cultivars that bloom longer than the wild varieties, making them even more enticing for the garden. Indigenous plants are also being cultivated to become more adaptable for planting further outside of their local habitats than their more stodgy, purebred native relatives.

Do you want to work with a cast member like this one?

This expanded group of native plants is also increasing the market for wildflowers and native plants beyond their home boundaries and into far-away lands where conditions are similar. For the most part, both cultivated garden plants and dressed-up natives will be good members of your garden troupe. However, there are some plants that have no manners at all and once introduced to a new venue simply lose all sense of proper behavior and invade all over the place.

There are invasive plants that have blustered in on the wind, stowed away on planes, or hitch-hiked down the freeways from one place to the next. Some have even used local wildlife as a means for transportation by offering seeds for food or clinging to fur coats. Invaders have been known to sneak into the pots of other plants or masquerade as different varieties. All too many have been bought and planted intentionally by the unsuspecting gardener who was enchanted by the plant's good looks, not realizing there was a monster lurking in those genes. Some people decided their imported plants no longer were welcome in their gardens so they dumped them into the wild to fend for themselves.

Whatever the reasons, many innocent-looking invaders have slipped into our gardens and out to the wild where they have multiplied with no shame. Plants like the decorative water hyacinth that garnishes the surface of a pond with its graceful inflated green and painted lavender flowers have escaped into the waterways in Florida and dammed up the water flow, choking the whole system and endangering both plants and animals. The ornamental Scotch Broom (*Cytisus scoparius*) that lights up in flower like a bright yellow flame capers all over Southern California scrub lands pushing out the native shrubs and offering nothing to feed the local chaparral birds. Purple Loosestrife is stalking wetlands all over the United States, gobbling up close to 475,000 acres a year! Even the ever-popular English ivy, *Hedera helix*, shuts out healthy woodland plants in the Northwest by smothering them with dense growth and shade. Some favorite garden plants have become

Beware: Invasive plants!
Photo by Barbara Black.

pests all over the world and many are still planted in areas where they shouldn't be introduced. You might notice that there are a respectable number of plants in the profiles listed in Chapter Six that have become villains in some parts of the planet. Some of these will even creep into your stonework, the foundation of your house, or pry through your windows! Think twice before planting an invader in your garden...no matter how pretty it looks in the pot.

Most of the aquatic plants can become problematic when introduced into areas where they are not native. With few natural controls on their growth, they can become rampant growers that will clog waterways. Be very careful when growing these plants in a water garden. However, because many are a good source of nutrition, they do make a great addition to the compost heap when they need thinning or removal — so opt for composting them rather than letting them loose in the local environment. If you choose plants that are not native to your area, you will need to take every precaution you can to grow all introduced plants so they remain in your garden.

Curiously enough, some evil villains in one geographical area are far better behaved thespians than they are in another. So it is important to do a little research before planting any non-native plant. Some of these invasive plants are okay if you are willing to care for them with proper pruning and deadheading. Some will be perfectly safe in the region where you live, but some will ruin the show for everyone. Before you even consider which plants you want to audition for your garden, check with your local agriculture department or call nearby universities with horticulture or botany departments to be sure you are hiring an acceptable cast member for your garden show. Although I am repeating this from the beginning of the book, I feel it bears repeating:

A good gardener these days must take responsibility for what he or she plants in the landscape.

summary:

The Garden, A Community

Plants have learned slowly over time to adjust to their surroundings to survive. Ordinarily, it is the Darwinian principle of evolution that gave the gift of passing on the most successful genes to those that survived environmental conditions. It's pretty simple stuff, but plants really just need conditions that will allow them to take up the necessary food, water, and light that will echo where their ancestor plants naturally developed. The majority of garden plants that people come into contact with have evolved in a part of this planet where conditions were not too extreme. Yet those conditions can still vary a lot. Plants can be at home in cool, shady forests or lust for the full, hot sun of a desert. The biggest trick to keeping your plants happy is to find out where they originally grew naturally and give them conditions that mimic their home environment. If you use a little plant logic, you'll see it really isn't all that difficult to figure out what conditions a plant needs. Just like in any performance, selecting the right talents that are comfortable in their roles will assure the best show possible.

Make your plants cozy in a familiar environment.

CHAPTER 3

MAKING MAINTENANCE EASY

Another reason people run into difficulties growing their plants successfully can be attributed to the human condition of always being busy with one thing or another. It's so easy to get distracted or simply not have time to fuss over the needs of those quiet members of the plant kingdom. All we have to do is pay a little more attention. Often our plants will tell us when we are amiss in our care, over-watering or under-watering, giving too much light or too little. The best way to make life easiest for both yourself and your plants is to set up systems that handle drainage, irrigation, lawn needs, wind and air issues, lighting, temperatures, and factor in sustainability. If a garden is created with systems and efficiency in mind, it is likely to maintain itself better. Then those occasional forgetful incidents will not take a disastrous toll on your garden performers.

Sometimes people think of plants as objects. A pretty plant is plunked down where it looks nice to the human eye, but for the plant, there may not be enough of the essentials it needs to grow in the chosen location. No matter how hard it tries to perform, it simply can't. On the other extreme, a plant may be so fussed over — being constantly watered, shoved into too much sun, or having its roots burnt from over feeding — that it is smothered and equally unable to put on much of a show.

People who kill plants from neglect often think they need to spend more time doting over their green-growing pals than may truly be necessary. There are plants that have very exacting demands that may be a challenge to grow well, but most plants are quite adaptable and forgiving. In fact, there are probably more plants grown indoors and out that are killed from too much attention than not enough.

Under-care vs. Over-care: Water

'More' is not always better. Plants that are drought-tolerant still need water to survive. Too much water will rot their roots. Food can sometimes give plants a boost or help make up for elements lacking in the soil. However, too much food will burn roots and kill the plant. The most important tool you can have is knowledge. Knowing your plants and your own garden will help you plant the right performer in the right place. You are far less likely to over-water a drought-tolerant plant if the soil is free-draining and you are less likely to dry-out a moisture-lover if the plant is planted where the soil stays damp. If you choose plants that like your soil just the way it is, you won't have to deal with feeding or worry about burning roots. Beware over-indulging your garden performers: you're not likely to get applause.

Under-care vs. Over-care: Light

Another sign of over or under-care can be inappropriate exposure. If you have plants that are growing pale or have long, thin, distorted growth, chances are your plant is suffering from *etiolation*. This is a condition in which plants are starving for light. No actor is happy about performing in the dark. You often see this in houseplants where conditions are extremely dark for plant life that evolved outdoors. The distortion is caused by weak growth and elongation to reach for more light. Paleness results from the lack of chlorophyll (chlorotic) due to low light. Symptoms will be cured by moving a plant slowly to more light. Light-starved plants should be introduced a little at a time to more light so they can begin normal food production. Suddenly moving a plant to lots of light can catch it unprepared and can cause the plant to burn.

The opposite problem of too little light is too much: burning. Plants given too much sun can look brown, black, or shriveled. They are literally being fried. This can happen easily when a plant that used to shade in a nursery or a home is suddenly moved into sunshine or plants outdoor suddenly lose the shade from an overhang or tree branch. Try to give your plant the amount of light it needs — not too much and not too little — and when moving plants, introduce them slowly to new conditions or give them some protection so they can adjust a little at a time.

~~~~~~~~~~~

The best way to avoid problems with under-care or over-care is to plant the right plant in the right location, set up systems to give that plant what it needs, and check over your plants regularly. That way you can see if problems are developing early on before they become serious.

SYSTEMS TO KEEP THE CAST PERFORMING

Setting up systems into your landscape is much like building the stage floor, backdrops, and lighting for a theatrical production. These are the parts of stagecraft that go unnoticed — unless there is a problem. For the actors, systems are usually taken for granted. Without a full-functioning stage to act out the play, much of the impact of the show is lost. Some people love setting up systems while others find it tedious, but the better functioning your systems, the healthier and happier your plants will be, the nicer they'll look, and the more time you'll save on maintenance. Also, good systems are the best way to keep your plants going when you forget. This is the more practical side of supporting your cast.

Setting up systems to improve conditions will make the necessary care automatic. The more you design your garden to care for itself, the less likely important needs will get overlooked. If you match your plants to the conditions in your property, you will need to give your garden minimal care and set up few, if any, systems. This would likely mean your garden would be designed with mostly local native plants or plants that naturally grow in very similar conditions. This is an ideal way of achieving a low-maintenance garden. Since local native plants might tend to grow weedy, though, designing needs to be done carefully before planting. Expect to prune and tie things up on a regular basis for crowd control. You can create a splendid garden with all native plants — one just as impressive as using out-of-town plants. It may take a little more planning and thought than just popping in a bunch of already-trained, cultivated imports to make it happen though. On the one hand, you will need less labor with watering, feeding, and drainage systems, but on the other, you will have to keep those wilder performers tamed so they stay within the roles of your garden design. Sorry, there is no such thing as a totally maintenance-free garden!

All-native gardens may be a great solution for the ecology and for low maintenance, but they don't appeal to everyone, especially since we have a long history of being conditioned to like anything but whatever is available in our own backyard!

If you want your plants to be happy and you are not expecting to use exclusively local native plants, then you will have to plan on giving your imported or cultivated cast members a little extra help. It's always easier for a good actor to ply his trade if he is given all the tools he needs, especially for more demanding roles.

Drainage is one of the most fundamental systems you'll need in your garden. Think of it as the supporting stage floor where your show will be taking place. No matter how good your script, actors, sets, and props may be, they need a properly functioning stage to perform on. Because drainage is one of the least romantic parts of landscaping, it's also an area all too often neglected. Don't be tempted to skimp on drainage systems. Not only will your plants complain, but you could create serious problems with your landscape and even your house if water builds up in the wrong places. Even before you start the final auditions for your plants, get your systems in place, starting with drainage.

Then you'll need to address irrigation, especially if you live where natural rainfall is not sufficient. You may also need systems to deal with wind and air circulation, potential lighting issues, and heat and cold concerns. The better preparation you put into your garden at the start, the easier it will be to maintain.

Native plants *can* make lovely gardens. Photo taken at the Santa Barbara Botanic Garden, Santa Barbara, California.

Drainage

Unlike plants, we are mobile, so we get to check out all the nooks and crannies of our properties. That means we can go on a scouting mission to decide what we want and where we want it in our landscape. That goes for both the living and non-living items. Take a little tour of your landscape area. Note the lowest points in your property. To assure water will flow into a drainage area, all general land surfaces should have a slope of at least two percent toward the lowest point(s).

In many parts of the country, home landscapes are being constructed with a swale — a depression in the landscape that forms a conduit for water to collect and flow either into a drainage channel or out into the street or other open area. In heavy rain, this swale should guide excess water away from your house or other structures. If no swale has been sculpted into your yard, then make a note of the natural low areas so you can turn them into places for water-collection. Not only will these low spots naturally fill up with wash water, but they will be perfect sites for placing entry grids for drainage pipes set below. In some places, a swale alone may be enough to keep the landscape well-drained, especially if you live where there is little rain. Any swale should be capable of handling the occasional downpour since even low-rainfall environments will experience sheeting rain now and again. You don't want that water inching up into your house.

However, don't be surprised if you need a full drainage system installed with the appropriate pipes and drains in the area where you live. It is not uncommon. Unless you know all about drainage, it would be wise to check with a professional before building your garden to find out what kind of drainage design is right for your property and climate. Drainage, like irrigation and utility systems, may not be the fun part of creating a landscape, but they are vital if you want to keep your home and finished garden in good condition.

Installing drainage is a critical part of a successful garden. In addition to drainage, irrigation and utility lines should go in before anything else in a new or redesigned garden. *Photo by Velvet Heller.*

Irrigation

Make irrigation as efficient and as automatic as possible to support your performers when they need it most: the extra effort and expense of creating a good system at the start will save you a lot more work and money later.

There are places in the world where nature is very generous with her rainwater and others where she supplies very little. At one time all living populations — plant, animal, and human — simply adapted to survival. Human civilization has changed all that and, as people thrive on the earth, they tend to form communities and those communities have expanded to huge populations in selected parts of the planet.

Large tracts of land have been terraformed to raise livestock, transformed into farmland, and paved over with tons of tar and cement. Cities have created micro-climates of their own and all this tampering has added complexity to the natural flow of nature. Weather patterns are shifting and stressing different parts of the world. How much is due to a natural change and how much is the direct impact of human civilization is beyond the scope of this book, but what

is not is the result: much land is being bent to demands for which it is not naturally suited and much of the weather is in conflict with those demands. Some of the more comfortable climates for people are areas where temperatures do not get very cold in the winter, so, with the ease of travel these days, these areas have become heavily populated with extreme demands on the natural water table. With the shifting intensity of drought, over-populated settlements are extracting water far faster than it can be replenished.

Plants would probably find this all quite bizarre if they could think since they naturally only populate a location so long as it can comfortably support their numbers, but we people have never let such boundaries deter us. Now we are facing the need to rethink our use of those basic water supplies. Water is one element life simply cannot survive without — even mankind. So the first place we can begin to control our water use is in the landscape. To use water without wasting it can have a big impact on extending our water supplies. After decades of warnings, it has finally become fashionable to design landscapes that are water-wise.

Drought tolerant gardening and efficient irrigation systems are becoming the new way to landscape in parts of the country. One way to water efficiently is to use a drip-irrigation system. Building a drip-irrigation is not difficult and it can be fun to put together.

The Show Must Go On

Water-wise gardens are trendy, beautiful, practical, and even low maintenance.

The construction of a watering system is rather like putting together a Lego® system. You choose all your parts and assemble them, one part added to the end of the next. It's pretty simple to do if you start out with a plan. If you just jump in, you are liable to end up with something that may not go where you want it to go.

Test your system when you are done installing it to make sure all of your plants are getting the water they need. The idea of a drip system is to allow a slow delivery of water over a period of time so the water can sink in deeply. Any spurts of water on the line should be fixed to allow for a slow application.

There are diverse choices in drip-irrigation tubing like those with laser cut emissions or sub-surface systems that are buried so they don't distract from the beauty of the garden. There are also a variety of drippers, sprinkler heads, soaker hoses, and other slow water delivery systems available. As the demand continues to grow for better watering methods, there are likely to be additional innovations in efficient watering systems.

Automatic irrigation controllers are the gardener's best friend when it comes to maintenance and memory assistance. These clocks allow you to set watering times in the landscape so you don't have to stand over your garden with a hose on a regular basis. Water timers can be as simple as little battery timers that you can program manually or digitally to allow a hose-driven system to turn water on and off for varied time periods. You can also set up a timed water control system that will regulate a number of valves so different parts of the landscape are watered at different intervals.

A little more expensive are the new 'smart controllers', which have sensors built in that detect changes in weather conditions and adjust accordingly. These 'smart' Weather-Based Irrigation Controllers (WBICs) gather their information from sensors in the landscape, at weather stations, and via satellite, the Internet, or even by microwave. Some base the watering needs on compiled data from previous years. There are different systems with different functions. Choose the one that best fits your garden and lifestyle, but expect that they will cost more than simple irrigation timers. Still, the extra cost of the controller will likely be offset by utility bill savings in a relatively short time.

These ET (evapotranspiration) controllers have been available for close to two decades, but are only now being designed for residential applications at affordable prices. Designs are still being refined, but, at the time of this writing, most of these systems are very efficient and can cost at least a couple hundred of dollars for a unit. Check with your city to see if there are any incentive rebates being offered that will make the initial cost a little less burdensome. Also, with the current fast growth of eco-friendly products for the garden, there are likely to be new designs coming on the market every year, pushing down the costs of previous models.

Part of efficient watering is as simple as checking out your landscape and watering systems regularly. You can tell pretty easily if you have a break in a water line or your sprinkler heads are sending water in the wrong direction spilling over walkways instead of delivering it where it is needed. Occasionally checking to see if your water is seeping into the soil and you aren't over-watering is another way to keep both waste and water bills down. By avoiding over-watering, you'll also be prolonging the lifetime of rock, soil, or concrete areas in your landscape that could be damaged over time by water runoff. Proper irrigation will help avoid erosion problems and garden plants will grow better.

Low-volume sprinkler heads are another way of making the best use of water in the garden. Gardens built on compacted, sandy, clay, or other soils that either resist absorbing water or let it drain through too fast have a hard time keeping the right moisture level around plant root systems. If the soil does not soak up the water as soon as it is applied, it will wash off or evaporate and be wasted. Water that is poured quickly into a fast-draining medium is likely to slither right past the root systems without giving plants a chance for a proper drink. You can help your soil by adding amendments like compost or other organics to help create a spongier texture. You can plant the kind of plant that loves the soil and climate you already have — in which case you'll need little or no irrigation anyway — or you can design an irrigation system that will deliver water slowly so it can seep into the soil rather than runoff, bypassing your plants.

For larger areas where versions of drip or soaker systems won't work, low-volume sprinkler heads are a good solution for distributing the water in smaller, lighter quantities than regular sprinkler heads. If you are delivering water more slowly then these systems will need to be on for a longer period of time. The concept is that a low-volume head that only puts out one-sixth the volume of an ordinary sprinkler head will still save water even if it needs to be left on for twice as long. You will save even more if you figure all of the water is likely to penetrate the soil instead of allowing much of the water (from the older designed watering head) to wash off unused.

As I said before, there are new designs being introduced regularly for more efficient irrigation systems. Look into which will best fit into your lifestyle, garden needs, climate, and budget. When it comes to budget, keep in mind that spending a little extra for a good quality irrigation system will end up paying for itself in water savings whereas a poorly made product that may be cheaper to buy initially might end up costing you more in time and money if you end up needing repairs and replacements.

THE FASHION OF LAWN

Humans like to think of lawns as being this big green blanket of sparkling, emerald green. In truth, a lawn is a community of lots of little, tiny green grasses — a mob of individual plants all snuggling up close together to make one big mass effect. We want our perfect lawns to march across the landscape with the tight regimen of single-bladed troops more numerous than the armies created by the best cinematic special effects. To that end we dump tons of water into our soils. Then we empty out bags and bottles of herbicides, insecticides, fungicides, and lawn foods — both synthesized and organic — all over our landscapes. We trim and weed and treat, and then fuss over our lawns. Once we are done spending all our money and effort on them, we are rewarded with the honor of spending more time and work carefully mowing all those little leaves in the ritual of making these thousands of little plants look like indoor carpeting.

The tradition of lawn is not as deep-rooted as people think. In fact, during the years that America was being settled, lawns were anything but common. It was the grand fashion during the first two decades of the twentieth century in England for landscapes to compete for the most lush, green sward. This worked well in places like the United Kingdom where soils were heavy with organics and rain was plentiful. It was a competition with this English landscape bravado that brought American designers into the style. Hybridizers tested out new strains of lawn grass to find ways to cultivate more locally friendly strains for planting in the United States. In some of the more southern climates endowed with generous rainfall, the large lawn found a comfortable home. The image of the grand southern mansion surrounded with acres of glowing green comes to mind. As the population increased all over the country, though, even desert, chaparral, and mountainous residential communities felt the pressure to pave their poorly adapted environments with lawns. As people move from one part of the country to another, it seems human nature that they want to bring the comforting memory of their childhood lawns with them. So it is that the lawn has become the default for any empty lot of land — and a very inappropriate default in some areas, indeed.

As the human population demands start depleting water resources even in some places that are not feeling the effects of a drought, it is finally becoming clear that water stewardship is necessary and

Do we really need these large lawns? *Photo by Barbara Black.*

thoughtlessly following traditions of a century past are neither wise nor stylish any more. Even if you are not focusing on the environmental impact of growing lawns, consider escalating water bills, and all the time and expense you'll be putting in just for the honor of having to mow your lawn regularly. Wouldn't it be nice to be able to live with the easy maintenance of minimal mowing or no mowing at all? Just think of all the more colorful or useful ways that space can be used other than carpeting it with a high maintenance green carpet. The possibilities are huge.

As you design the stage for your garden show and cast the different performers, give some thought to the role you want to fill for ground-cover. In defense of lawns, grass ground-cover still has plenty to offer for play areas, picnic spots, or other practical applications. Lawns do help purify toxins in the air as do all living, green-growers. If you choose to grow and care for a lawn, make sure you use the right variety for your environment and install the best systems you can to maintain your lawn — watering, feeding, aerating, de-thatching, cutting, and edging. Make sure you are using lawn where it performs best aesthetically and practically.

Replacement Choices for Lawn

Where lawns do not earn their living there may be better alternatives. Although it does

Lawn replacement can taste great. This lettuce is a more edible form of green. *Photo by Velvet Heller.*

Bonsai plants were developed to echo the natural dwarfing of trees that are stunted by the harsh, exposed slopes in Japan. Photo taken at the Japanese Garden at the Tillman Reclamation Plant, Van Nuys, California. *Photo by Velvet Heller.*

require a lot of watering, replacing a lawn with a vegetable garden may be a better use of space. At least you will get healthy, tasty edibles for your water investment.

You could also make your property easy-care or more colorful by replacing a lawn with native gardens or handsome, low-growing ground-cover plants that offer colorful flowers or interesting textures. Other possibilities might be to use non-living materials like stone, gravel, brick, pavers, and, yes, where it makes sense, maybe even synthetic grass. There are many kinds of ground-cover choices available today that can help us design really fabulous-looking landscapes that fit our individual environments. Don't just automatically jump into automatic gear and opt for filling up space with an out-dated fashion from a century ago. Think about the best solution for your own garden that will use water wisely, create a more interesting garden design and save you a lot of labor in maintenance.

AIR AND WIND EFFECTS

Good air is one of the basic necessities for growing a happy garden. There needs to be good air circulation and plants need their breathing pores (stomata) to be clean so they can breathe just like us. Air temperatures need to be within the boundaries of where different plants have evolved and winds need to be taken into consideration, too.

Some plants grow smaller and stouter in response to windy conditions. Plants that have not evolved this way may not be able to adapt and can blow over or simply die away if planted in high-wind conditions. You can help protect less adapted plants with walls, cloches, stakes, and other protections.

The materials you use for plant supports can even be part of your scenic effects in your garden show. Consider using bamboo stakes with a tropical look. Build a rustic scene with a rough-hewn stone wall that will block winds while mediating temperatures — by slowly releasing the heat of daytime sun at night and doing the same with the nighttime cool when the morning warmth rises. Use an interesting slatted roof to allow gentle air flow while creating a contemporary set design that houses delicate plants. Air and wind effect controls are somewhat informal systems to help minimize seasonal changes or protect vulnerable areas in your landscape. They probably would match up with the placement of furniture on a theatrical set.

STAGING YOUR LIGHTING

Give your plants the light they need to grow. Indoor plants may need the aid of grow lights to supplement the infrared and ultraviolet rays frequently denied in the low light of indoor growing. Shade-lovers can benefit from the natural shadows created by being planted on the north-facing side of your outdoor garden or under an awning or tree. Make sure the sun-lovers get all the solar power they can by checking out light and shade patterns created in your garden as the sun moves across the sky. If you live in a hot-summer climate, planting a shade tree on the south-facing or west-facing side of your house will cool your home. The shade can also lower your air-conditioning bills by about ten percent, but make sure you place your young tree carefully. The time of year will also change the direction of the shadow. Don't wait for five or ten years only to find out you were off a bit in your planting and the shade misses the house altogether in the hottest sun of the summer! Use a compass at planting time.

Let Mother Nature help light your garden show. You can not only keep your plants happy by locating them where they will get the proper lighting, but you can even get special effects with natural lighting.

Use a little artistic flair — stage your lighting by planning areas to be silhouetted by the early rising or setting sun. Large, sculptural plants can cast dramatic shadows if placed where the sunlight throws shadows against flat, simple surfaces. Fine, feathery foliage or blossoms can glow if planted where sunlight gleams through them. Factor in the glitter of sunlight off of water in your landscape with water gardens, fountains, or waterfalls. Use both sun and shade to create your own special effects in the garden.

The Effect of Man-made Lighting

By becoming familiar with your garden's topography, you can figure out how water will run in rains or with irrigation. By taking the time to see how the sun affects

Landscapes become magical when lit up at night. *Photo by Velvet Heller.*

different parts of your garden at diverse times of the year, you can better choose the right location for your garden performers and design in optical effects. You can also take these natural systems one step further by adding man-made lighting after dark to emphasize the theatrical effect of your landscape.

Night lighting with solar, low-volt, or LED lights will dramatically bring your garden show to life after dark. You can use up-lighting, down-lighting, back-lighting, spotlights, and decorative light fixtures to turn your garden into a mystical fairyland at night. Some lighting can perform double-duty as a safety feature to pick out steps or pathways. Lights can feature clumps of plantings or special garden décor to create a nighttime focal point. If you plan to keep your garden performance going into the dark hours, you may also want to audition some night-blooming, perfumed, or white-flowered plants that will add dimension to the evening show.

Most plants are not affected by lights at night, though there are a few that need long periods of uninterrupted dark to set flowers — like the Poinsettia or the Chrysanthemum. However, these can be moved if planted in pots or covered if they are directly impacted by lighting. Apart from these rare exceptions, both plants and people can benefit by extending your garden show into the evening hours. A dramatic nighttime garden show will provide an excellent excuse to spend more time outdoors alone or with friends, family, and neighbors to enjoy the garden performance after dark.

DIRECTING TEMPERATURES

Creating a system to control the weather has been the stuff of science fiction for generations and thus far we haven't been very successful. However, you can build systems into your garden that will make maintenance easier with subtle temperature variations.

Cold runs like water and will pool in lower spots. If you want to create a warmer area in your garden, you can create a barricade to the flow of cold. Just imagine the surface of your landscape as if water were running over it. Picture where the water would collect and where it would miss. Hills are the easiest to deal with as you can imagine the cold rolling down the slope. If you created a wall part way down, the cold would build up behind the wall whereas the area in front of the wall on the lower side would remain a little warmer and protected.

Walls are one form of hardscape, which is the term for solid or permanently-built features in the landscape. Using different construction materials can also form part of an informal temperature regulation system. Dense materials like cement and stone work like temperature mediators. When they are exposed to warmth, they slowly heat up. Unlike lighter materials that have more air in their composition, these will take a while to absorb heat; likewise, when the temperatures cool, stone and cement will take a lot longer to chill down. As a result, dense building materials will stay warmer as temperatures fall and cooler as the outside air heats up. By surrounding gardens or individual plants with hardscapes made of dense materials, you will be radiating heat and cold that will help create a mini-environment where temperatures will take longer to change, giving vulnerable plants some protection from dangerous heat and cold spikes. You cannot alter your whole climate this way, but you can mitigate some of the more sudden temperature changes. Eventually, the overall seasonal temperatures will prevail.

Other ways of dealing with extremes of heat or cold can be done with physical protections like shade covers, planting under trees, overhangs, or even moving potted plants into protected areas like greenhouses, sun rooms, porches, or into the house. Although protection from radical air temperature changes can be factored into your landscape design, this is a system in the most informal use of the term. By adding provisions to mediate the weather, especially during extreme or unexpected events, you will make the job of caring for your garden easier on yourself and increase the chance of your plants surviving the odd challenges that might otherwise destroy them. This is the garden version of having the set design and scenery not only support but also protect the performers.

SUSTAINABLE LANDSCAPING

Old ideas are dressing up as new systems. Despite all our new technology, we are beginning to realize that there is merit to a number of the old ways of doing things. Mixing new technology and old ideas can make gardening more efficient.

Theatrical productions are masters of efficiency. The stage is a small space that needs to offer the illusion of reality by manipulating sets, costumes, lighting, sound, actors, and props to bring to life the words written in a script. There is no room for waste and frivolity, yet the impression can often be one of excess. Illusion is the skill of good stagecraft. Gardens can learn a lot from getting the most out of every bit of design, feature, plant, and piece of décor. Efficient landscaping can be created with recycling materials, getting double-duty out of construction design, and using what nature has already provided.

"Sustainable" and "Eco-friendly" are some of the most fashionable words these days. It's interesting since these are some of the oldest techniques in the history of gardening. In our deep, dark past, humans were completely dependent on the ecology around them for survival and there was no illusion of man being superior to Mother Nature, nor was it practical for individuals to live life isolated from the land. As the wear and tear

of the planet begins to impact individuals, humanity is collectively beginning to embrace ideas that have been on the market for a long, long time. Sustainable gardening has finally come back into demand and with it come a whole supply of new businesses and freshly designed products. The subject has enough material for plenty of additional books. Yet there are possibilities worth mentioning here to get you thinking about ideas and systems that you can factor into your garden show to make the whole thing play out easier.

"Sustainability" means that by setting up much of your garden to flow with the natural conditions all around it, you will have to intercede less. That's essentially what this whole book is about — from the planting point of view, anyway. Since people are

Sustainable landscaping can be even more decorative than traditional methods. Vertical gardening can make dull walls into hanging gardens, show pieces or even edible walls. *Photo by Diane Sullivan.*

rarely impressed with what they already have, we simply must bring in the alluring and slightly harder to attain. Thus we import plants, building materials, and other parts of our landscape. It's simply our nature to want to control our surroundings while making them, well, a little different than everyone else's surroundings. That's why a lot of folks are not really thrilled with creating a completely local native garden.

However, we can blend the local plants and materials with some eye-catching additions — like introducing the more dramatic events in a play — and then we can smooth the transitions with eco-friendly systems that make it all flow together. One of the major reasons people have trouble growing a successful garden is that they just get busy and either forget or don't have time to pamper their plants. So, once again, making your life flow with natural and human-devised systems will make your chances of having a successful garden show much greater. No one has ever complained that they didn't like their garden because it was too easy to care for!

Sustainable systems can be set up for water by collecting and recycling rainwater. There are systems that offer underground storage tanks, rain barrels, purification ponds, and bog or rain gardens. Permeable paving and vertical gardening make the most of space and allow the earth to breathe without wasting water. Recycling everything from old stone, broken curbing and cement, wood, glass, and old tires has created new products with interesting patinas and handsome effects. Re-purposing materials has cut down on building material budgets and encouraged do-it-yourself building while slowing the growth of our landfill areas. It has even saved money for many a homeowner who reused something rather than buying new.

Energy can be stored from wind and solar collectors in large systems or the smallest little products. These natural energy storage devices can save on utility bills, upkeep, and reduce waste. When you put together your landscape, check out some of the newer inventions that use naturally renewable resources.

Keep sustainability in mind as you read the next chapter on putting all the pieces of your garden show together. Your living plants need a healthy, safe place to grow if you want them to perform well. They are even more dependent on their 'stage' than actors in a play. Blend the right plants with the right landscape design and materials and then combine the results with practical, embedded systems (natural or otherwise) to help you keep things running smoothly while you're busy with your own life. A great garden performance will take work, but you should still have plenty of time left over to enjoy the show.

Set your stage with the right basics like proper drainage systems and put together a healthy environment with the plants that are best adapted to the offered conditions. Like everything in life, if you start with a good foundation, everything built from then on tends to look better and last longer. Set up a good foundation for your garden by dealing with structural problems at the start: if you build the framework solidly and add efficient systems, not only will the living parts of your landscape thrive but also your job of maintenance will be less costly in time and money. When things are set up to roll along smoothly, you don't have to worry about forgetting any of the essentials. Try to check on drainage, soil, water, and light systems every now and again to catch breakages or malfunctions early on. Other than that, doing a thorough job of preparation will pay back handsomely in the performance of your garden.

Summary:
Expectations

Always be fair to your plants and yourself. Never has there been a Broadway production in which every last detail has gone perfectly. In fact, it has to be a very large problem for an audience to even notice when something does go wrong. Once your garden is playing out its seasonal scenes, chances are that you will likely be the only one to notice when certain areas don't look the way you want.

Even when it comes to the blatant problems, you need to be realistic. Human nature is such that even though we know that a perfectly beautiful-weather day is an exception to the rule, we still expect every day to measure up to our ideal expectation that all days should be lovely. We know the expectation is ridiculous, but we keep hoping anyway.

No landscape or garden is ever perfect. We expect our gardens to look like the photographs in calendars, magazines, and other media, but take a closer look at some of those photographs. You just might find a flower blooming out of season or a sun-lover blooming happily in deep shade. Sometimes, if you search carefully enough, you may even see the rim of the pot where this imported plant was set to fill the hole in the photograph with just the right bit of color to make the picture 'perfect'. You might discover the ideal pond in the composition you are studying is actually supporting some gaily blooming plastic water lilies or the background near a fence line has been stuffed with baskets of silk foliage. Photographers set their stages, too.

Even if you find yourself envious of a particularly showy stretch of garden in your local arboretum or while touring a private garden, remind yourself these glamorous spaces have a full-time crew of gardeners preening them and replacing any plant that isn't pretty enough to be on stage. You can wander around your own garden in the growing season and likely find at least one angle, plant, or scene that will make an impressive photograph even if the rest of your garden is looking poorly.

In short, a garden is a living thing. No living thing is perfect. Perfect is dull and boring. The beauty of your garden is that it is always in a state of transition. Like the Broadway play, scenes will change, some parts work better than others, and these are both arts that are perpetual works-in-progress. That's one of the gifts of creating art with life. There is always the unexpected, change, and variety. Don't set yourself up for disappointment by expecting your garden to be perfect — ever. It's not fair to you or your plants. Instead, make the best scenes you can, help your garden residents grow strong and healthy, and delight in the surprises your garden will offer you. The perfect garden is an illusion mostly concocted to sell products and to promote the impossible fantasy. There is no perfect garden — and that's actually a good thing. Perfection is perfectly dull.

Putting Together the Show (Garden)

CHAPTER 4

Whether you are putting together a garden, a theatrical show, or any other project, there are multiple pieces that all go together to create the final product. In any job, the design you follow, the foundation you lay, and the materials you use will determine your ultimate success. Start with a well-thought out plan, integrate solid design elements, add the right softscape (living materials) and hardscape (non-living and permanent materials), and your garden will give you a rave review show.

Although this book has focused mainly on the living performers in your garden, the best show will only take place if you put all the elements of the production together. You can choose the best actors, put them in the best-dressed garden beds, and get a superb performance out of them, but your garden needs to read as a whole play with all the parts working together to create a unified show. This chapter will help you order the parts of your landscape and make them flow together visually as well as support each other practically.

BASIC STAGE DESIGN

You can try to adapt your property to the profiles of the plants you like or you can make your life much easier by selecting plants that will blend into your space naturally. Think in terms of putting on that garden show again. Any successful piece of artwork is comprised of different parts that work harmoniously to create a whole. You will want the stars of your landscape production to stand out as the focal point of your garden, but stars need supporting roles. Back-up can come from the kind of plants that surround your focal point. Grouped plants can form secondary themes or create a supporting 'chorus'. Even the 'walk-on roles' — the minor plants that do not attract attention to themselves — form part of the overall mood of the garden.

Don't ignore the need for quiet spaces. Just as you do not want the stage to be constantly overwhelmed with busy actors, moments of quiet and contrast are necessary to hold interest. Quiet areas may be as simple as ground-cover plants, lawn, or maybe even no plants at all. Putting together an interesting overall landscape design is much like writing the play itself: if you don't have a form and flow that leads from one scene to the next, there will be nothing to anchor anyone's attention. Once you have a good basic design, each main part of your design can become an act in your play. That means that you will want to design sets for each scene of your act. Think of this in terms of creating hardscapes — permanent features like patios, pools, walls, fountains, and practical areas like driveways, walkways, and outdoor rooms. As your play unfolds, different scenes are acted out by the living elements: the plants you choose. These

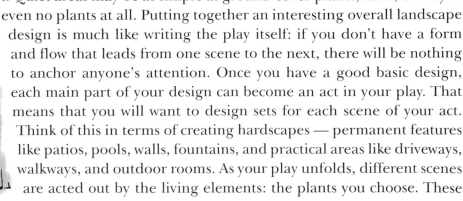

The décor in this landscape establishes the theme and mood for the garden. It becomes the center around which the whole design is built. *Photo by Velvet Heller.*

can play major roles like shade trees or walk-on parts like annual filler plants.

Don't forget the props. Every presentation is enriched with some little bit of extra interest. Add an old wheelbarrow planted with trailing flowers that spill over the edge, a decorative piece of sculpture, or a brightly colored trellis with a clambering, flowering vine to contrast with a blank wall. Garden décor can add even more interest to your garden show.

The materials, features, and décor not only lay out the look of your garden, but they can perform double-duty, too. Stone or concrete patios can help

A bridge can become an artistic feature of a landscape design while guiding traffic over a ravine or other area that is difficult to cross. Photo taken at the Holland Residence.

minimize the fluctuations of air temperatures for nearby plants. Set up retaining walls so they can be used as attractive benches for seating. Cover a dreary wall with cheerful vines that can also produce edible fruits or colorful blooms for flower arrangements. Cross a ravine or a waterway with a bridge that makes a decorative statement as well as offering convenient passage. Think about how all the parts of your design can work together to get the most out of your total garden presentation.

PLANNING THE DESIGN

It's important to audition the right plants for your garden show. The materials and décor of your set also need careful selection. How do you put these elements together? It's all about design. A good design is like the main script of a play that develops plot, characters, and gives stage descriptions and directions. A design will be the plan you follow to create your whole show. Whether you are going to design your garden by yourself, consult with a professional, or have that professional do the whole job for you, there are some guidelines that should help you put the design together.

Start with a plan. Whether you scribble your garden design out on a napkin or do a to-the-inch, architectural rendering, putting it down on paper is likely to create the most important tool you can have for creating a successful garden. Doing a design is something you can do by yourself or with help. You can sketch out your ideas on a piece of paper, lay out a plan with computer software, work with a professional garden designer or landscape architect, or have one of these professionals do the design for you. Whatever method you use, don't skip this step. It's very hard not to make at least a few mistakes when planning out your garden and if you make those errors on a drawing, it's much easier and cheaper to make changes with an eraser or delete key than it is to deal with them when you are paying for labor and materials. You also can see which design ideas will work better on paper and research how different construction materials will look.

Failure to do a design plan is considered the number one worst mistake commonly made in landscaping. It can also be the most expensive. Although hiring design help is not inexpensive, the savings in future disasters — misplaced trees ripping up building foundations, plants being replaced over and over, features like hot tubs or barbecues placed where they are inconvenient or downright dangerous — can be well worth the investment up-front.

Preparing your design is easier if you follow steps. Wander your property and look at it from all angles. Pay special attention to the views of your garden from windows looking out from the house or any vantage point where you want to emphasize or block a view. Take notes on a quick sketch of your yard.

Note micro-climates on your sketch: again, like water, cold rolls down hill and pools against barriers and low spots, so you can plan on these areas being cooler than other areas of your garden. Label areas where there are existing structures that will retain heat and cool or offer shade or other forms of protection to plant life. Sketch out locations where you want to place permanent features.

Next you will want to plan out systems like drainage and irrigation. Factor in electrical and gas lines making sure you plan on more than you are likely to need. You can always stub in utility lines and cap them if you don't need them yet. If you set your systems in place all at once, it will be easier and less expensive than adding them later. Retrofitting may require that you destroy parts of your finished garden to extend systems you could have roughed in earlier. The extra pipes will cost comparatively little even if you never end up using them.

Lay out the events in your garden. Make sure to consider practicalities. For example, you will want to locate a vegetable garden where it is reasonably close to your kitchen so it is convenient for cropping edibles. Place a compost heap close enough to make it usable, but far enough away that you don't invite rodents to move in close to your home. Another example might be to locate an outdoor spa close enough to your house or to a cabaña

where there is quick access to dry towels and warmth for bathers when they get out of the toasty water and into the cool air. Consider adding steps to different levels or ramps for easy passage for wheel barrels, bicycles, walkers, wheelchairs, or any other rolling items.

Design Around a Focal Point

One of the best ways to create a 'plot' to the story of your garden is to design a focal point into the layout. Just as a good storyline has peaks of excitement, your garden can provide visual interest by using contrasting events. All you need to do is create one main event that catches the eye to anchor your garden. A focal point is essential to a good design whether you are designing a room, painting a piece of artwork, or creating a landscape. The focal point will serve like the climax of your garden story.

You can create more than one focal point, but consider secondary focal points to be lesser supports for your main event. Don't add competing focal points that take away from the main feature and confuse the composition. Consider points of interest that are less riveting than your main focal point to be like supporting roles in a play: they help build the overall story and support the main event. Focal points can be living or not, a single object or a grouping. You can use rocks and boulders, constructs or sculptures, fountains or logs. Focal points can underscore a theme, like a carved tree-trunk bench in a woodland garden, an unusual specimen banana tree in a tropical garden, or a wagon wheel in a rustic Western landscape. Consider a showy seating area with unusually shaped, colored, or styled furniture as a focal point. Lead up to your focal point with paths, garden beds, fencing, or decorative border materials. Invite entry with an archway or an unexpected gateway to a fence. Sometimes adding a surprise feature can become a focal point in itself.

Creating a focal point can be one of the more fun parts of designing the landscape. You can use a favorite item, search through garden centers, check out your attic, garage, or wander through a junk yard and find a creative way to recycle some object into a focal point. Or you can plant an exciting area with

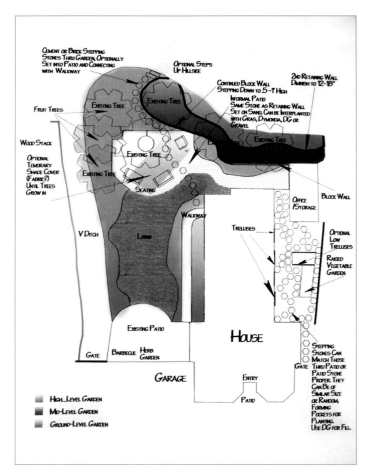

Always start with a plan on paper! This one is done on a computer, but you can draw plans by hand, too.

Putting Together the Show (Garden)

A graceful Japanese Maple becomes the focal point for this Asian garden. It is supported both literally and artistically by secondary focal points of rocks and the lantern décor. Photo taken at the Hannah Carter Japanese Garden.

some really showy specimen plants to create drama in your garden design. Living focal points will shift and change with time, but with careful planning you can have an area of plants performing in one season and, when they finish flowering, have the focus shift to another attention-getting focal point with different blooming plants. This kind of performance might be better compared to a musical performance where the emphasis shifts from the woodwinds to the brass, moves to the strings, and maybe slips back to the woodwinds again in an orchestral composition. There are many ways to design your landscape elements to complement each other. Just make sure you don't overdo it. Any good design has elements of peace and quiet to off-set the areas of activity.

Add in special feature areas like sport courts, pet enclosures, entertainment areas, or vegetable gardens. Don't forget the practicalities, either. Factor in access for maintenance and convenience: tool sheds, gates, and utility areas. Visualize how all the events in your garden will look and relate to each other in the landscape as a whole. All this will be easiest done on a drawing where you can play around with the pieces before you commit to where they will go.

A Few Design Tips

There are three basic principles that will help you layout a good-looking design
and make your landscape flow together visually.

1. ODD NUMBERS WORK BEST.

I have no idea why, but truly they do. Ones and threes work great for larger objects and fives can work for smaller items. Don't space single 'ones' equidistantly unless you want to intentionally create a pattern. You can break up larger areas into groupings. They just look more natural than setting things in two's and fours. You can certainly break the rule every now and then, but try not to make designs look too predictable. Avoid straight lines, symmetrical, and evenly-spaced items unless you are creating a stylistic, contemporary effect. Straight little rows of flowers in a natural garden look ridiculous and no natural dry riverbed ever formed in a perfectly straight line. Only use geometric, exact, balanced designs for formal landscape effects.

2. STICK TO A COLOR SCHEME.

Choose colors that blend or contrast well with your home. Too many colors in the garden will create a feeling of unease and confusion. You can do a single color theme by using different plants that all bloom in, say, all reds or all whites. Or you can plan a garden in warm colors — reds, oranges, and yellows — or cool — pinks, purples, and blues. Whites tend to pop brightly in shade gardens because they contrast with the darker shadows. Dark colors speak of mystery. Pastel shades offer a sense of softness. Interesting effects can be created with a single color family used throughout the garden with a contrasting shade of color designed as a carefully placed accent. Colors can be painted into your hardscape on wood, stucco, or metal with paints, varnishes, or stains. Cement can be colored with tints or acid stains and even natural stone comes in a wide range of colors. Add color accents with bright or printed fabrics for outdoor furniture, pillows, or drapes. Snap attention to an unnoticed corner with a brilliant, eye-catching ceramic pot. Or paint a blank fence or wall with a mood-setting tone or an interesting mural. Use color in your landscape. Bright colors will add a feel of energy whereas muted colors will create relaxation. Color can be a powerful tool in setting the theme and mood of your garden show.

3. USE GROUPINGS.

A garden with events or plants spotted all over will not flow as a total picture. Little events fighting against each other do not create a unified whole. Like any good show, one thing needs to lead to the next with special features highlighted. Several rocks together will grab interest much better than an odd rock placed here and there for no particular reason. Activity contrasts well next to inactivity. This means that if you look at your garden as a whole, you should be able to see areas of peacefulness where there is little happening, like a lawn, a gravel area, or a ground-cover space. Your eye can then be drawn by paths or small objects that will lead you to the main event: your focal point. Maybe there will be more supporting areas of interest that might lead you back to peacefulness or even to another, greater focal point. You want your whole garden to read like a painting or like a story. Let the events of your garden take you on a tour. This works for plants, too. Areas of bloom or colorful foliage will attract the eye. Backdrops of a single type of plant will be effective to offset a busier garden in the foreground. Tall, sword-shaped foliage will give vertical interest to a garden of all rounded mounds. Your garden can tell a visual story. It needs contrast and continuity. Repeat materials and plants in your design so the garden keeps its unique personality.

Putting Together the Show (Garden)

Grouping plants, events, and décor will combine with color themes and basic, good design to put on the whole show you want from your landscape. Just as actors, sets, and props all work together with a good script to present a successful play, look at your garden as a whole comprised of all its parts. Once your design is laid out and works aesthetically and practically you will have your stage set for your cast of character plants.

Design in the Cast of Plants

Audition and select your plants for where they will both look and grow best. Plan the best positions to grow your starring roles and design the supporting roles around your stars. Think in terms of the softscape (living plants) as the action to your hardscape (permanent structures). Your plants will change throughout the seasons as they grow. Always plant your young plants in a space as if they were full-grown — because they will need every inch of that space to fill their natural character profile. Too often a cute little tree of six feet tall will look perfect in the spot you choose only to turn into a sixty-foot giant in less than a decade, prying up concrete with its roots and bashing walls with its branches!

To have a successful show, *again* think about how your plants will vary throughout the year. All areas of your garden will change. A focal point of a showy flowering shrub will fade to dullness when it has finished performing its scene just as its surrounding plants will rise and fall in showiness. You can benefit by designing a chorus of later-flowering plants to surround your lead character so they can sing through the gap while the lead character is in the process of a costume change.

Colorful flowers are only one type of show that plants can put on in your garden. Fruit and berries can be ornamental and leaves can add form, shape, and texture — and some of them are as brightly colored as flowers. Even textured and colored tree bark can be sculptural and add interest in any season. Plan for autumn foliage colors, too. Once you have chosen your cast of plants and you know they will perform well in your garden conditions, you become the director and choreographer of your landscape design. Think of early blooming bulbs to add a riot of color when springtime first arrives and so many of the other garden flowers are just yawning back to life. When the bulbous plants have finished their display, let them die back without trimming the foliage so the energy can go down and be stored away to make new bulbs for next years' flowering. That's the perfect time to tuck the yellowing foliage behind those later-blooming plants that are finally coming into flower.

Making the parts of your garden blend into a single, successful production means you want all the parts to help support each other. Don't forget about your design basics of using odd numbers, color coordination, and grouping. It is easy to fall in love with too many plants for a limited garden space and end up with one of everything. If you do that, your show will have no storyline. You need to repeat groups of the same kind of plant throughout your garden for continuity.

A swimming pool is a practical feature that can become a major focal point in your overall garden design. *Photo by Velvet Heller.* (Naturalized pool design by Nick Williams.)

SUPPORT YOUR CAST & THEY'LL SUPPORT YOU

Sets and Décor in the Garden

Today property is more than just the land that surrounds a house. We are now using our yard space as an extension of the household living area. We want to be able to participate in the use of a landscape, which makes it even more important that our outdoor surroundings are attractive enough to entice us outside to make use of that space...that we are invited into the garden show.

The setting of the landscape then becomes more than just a stage for our botanical friends to perform. It expands to an inviting place for people to play, grow food, exercise, entertain, or use as a peaceful retreat from all the pressures of daily life. As you design your landscape, you may want to include some major features that make the garden an important part of your life or that of your family. Think in terms of some of the following structures to include when setting the stage for your landscape:

Outdoor room(s)
Swimming pool and/or spa
Vegetable garden
Built-in barbecue
Meditation or reading garden nook
Dining area
Picnic area
Outdoor chimney, fire pit, oven, or chimney
Exercise or sports area
Children play areas (a tree house?)
Work or hobby space
Pet pens and runs
Potting shed and garden work area
Chicken coops or stock animal enclosure
Golf putting green
Gazebo
Fruit tree orchard
Pond or water garden
Statue(s)
Boulders and rocks
Dry river stream
Waterfall/Fountain

This is just a partial list to get you thinking of all the fun and useful items that can be built into the outdoor garden. If your space is limited, go for small features. Don't try to put too much into your space or it will look cluttered and confusing. If you want to use more than one feature, plan it out so one thing leads to the next in a comfortable flow using pathways, garden areas, or maybe stepping stones. Small items are best grouped. Larger items are best seen as focal points. If you have the space, you can create hidden gardens so more than one feature can be included without visually battling another.

Décor can add the finishing touches to your garden performance or, in this case, a bit of whimsy and a bold, artistic statement. (Sculpture by David Rogers at the Santa Barbara Botanic Garden, California.)

Add some surprise with something like this hidden dinosaur peeking through foliage. *Photo by Velvet Heller.*

Use décor to set the mood, emphasize a theme, or accentuate a special spot. Décor would be small items like lamps, colorful cushions or outdoor drapes, small sculptures, trellises, archways, wind chimes, or fancy stepping stones. Keep to a color theme with your décor. Try not to collect too many items or just plunk them anywhere. If you love to collect small objects, you might want to create a special garden area just to display them rather than strewing them all over the stage to trip up performers and audiences alike.

Sustainability and recycling are part of the new tools that are re-entering today's gardening approach. Systems like permeable paving and water collection provide opportunities for creating form and patterns as well as new planting areas. Growing space expands into "green" roofs, doffing the heads of cement skyscrapers in the cities, barns and sheds in the country, and backyard rooftops in the suburbs. Your choices of plants will depend on where you live, but there is no reason you can't insulate a detached guest house, a garage, or a backyard shed with a grassy roof in moist climates or paint them with the colorful shapes and forms of low-growing succulents in hot, dry areas. Patches of green are appearing on the flat tops of the tallest urban buildings where gardens offer an escape from the daily pressures while recycling rainfall and adding insulation to the top floor of high-rise constructions.

If you have only a small space for gardening, look into creating vertical walls. You can grow vegetables, herbs, or flowers up the side of a block wall, hang specially adapted natural blankets of planting pockets along a wooden fence, or create free-standing living walls made of a grid work of little containers that can be filled with soil and plants that are decorative, edible, or both.

The possibilities for creating exciting, lovely gardens are limited only by our imaginations. "All the garden's a stage" and that stage is incorporating our plant friends and people together in a whole new scenario of plots and designs.

Extra Prompting on Growing Plants

Keep your plant players rehearsed and in top performing condition. Even when you have done your homework and gotten to know which plants are likely to do well in your garden, there are a few directing tips that might help you have more success in your garden.

What is the source for your plant characters? If you are propagating by seed or cuttings, chances are

your plants will naturally acclimate to their surroundings as they grow. If you are transplanting a plant from another area, chances are that it is used to slightly different conditions and will need extra care to adapt. If you have dug your transplant, there is probably considerable root damage so expect the plant to suffer some setback from shock. If you bought your plant at a retailer, it's likely that plant was raised in controlled, radically different conditions. Many garden centers ship plants in from all over the country, sometimes from all over the world.

Don't be surprised if your plants have been grown in large greenhouses under specially maintained, ideal conditions to allow for mass production. These plants may not be used to the vagaries of dry or wet air, wind, direct sunshine, or the range of temperatures encountered in outdoor living. Local garden centers are more likely to be carrying locally grown plants or, if there isn't a large, fast turnover, their plants may have had some time to acclimate to outdoor living right there in the nursery lot. Plants that have been grown in similar conditions to your own will settle in faster than those that have to deal with more stressful environmental changes — whether they are native varieties or not.

If you are not sure about the background of your recent purchase, it's always wise to give your new arrival(s) a chance to 'harden off'. This means that if you can place the new plant in its container for at least a few days in the exact spot where it will be planted, you will be giving it a chance to get used to its new home before it goes through the additional stress of being knocked out of the pot and set into new soil.

I repeat: give your garden players a little extra care when they first join your troupe. If you live where the sun is bright or hot, a little extra shading will be welcome. If you live where the soil drains fast, give your plant extra water until its roots have spread sufficiently to support it in the drier soil. Even the toughest of plants will need your help adjusting to a major move. Consider that most plants go through damage and shock when they are planted or moved. Fine root hairs that you don't see are often broken during planting. By giving your new plants a little boost when they move in, you are increasing their chance of growing happily into their new homes.

Oh, and by the way, this does not mean to give them food. Plants are not people and will not heal faster with chicken soup — even 'chicken soup' formulated for plants. Food is something that can help boost plant growth after it is established. Feeding when plants are stressed is likely to do more damage than good, so just be gentle with your new arrivals and welcome them by protecting them from extremes. They'll let you know if you are doing it right by perking up more and more each day as they settle into their new homes.

LET THE SHOW BEGIN

Once your garden is designed and built — complete with any special features, your systems in place and tested, and your plants auditioned, selected, and planted — your garden show is ready to be enjoyed.

There will always be maintenance. Things wear out and break. Plants die. Systems malfunction or need tweaking. A landscape is a living thing and it will change over time. Expect that even with the most rigid auditioning you will still lose some plants. It may not be your fault at all. Sometimes plants, like people, have weak genetic programming. Sometimes a plant that should thrive simply refuses and then there are always those few plants that should not do well where planted and grow like a weed just for spite. Like all rules, there will be exceptions — and usually the least expected ones, too.

Plan on doing regular check-ups on your garden. Not only will you catch little problems before they become big ones, but it is soul-soothing to wander around your garden and inspect how Mother Nature

has decided to interpret the script you've set out. You will also discover that Mother Nature loves to ad-lib, so expect lots of uninvited weeds to take advantage of the cozy environment you've created. Plan on insects trundling in and dropping out of the sky. Underground eating machines like gophers and moles may tunnel in to dine on your favorite performers and other wildlife will hop, lope, slither, sneak, and saunter in to feed off of your generous offerings.

The wildlife you find in your garden will depend much on where you live. In some cases you may have to take action to protect your garden show. For some reason, most wildlife has never really grasped the concept of sharing nor do they have the decency to leave thank you notes after decimating your garden. On the one hand, if you are keeping your native wildlife happy, you have probably created a pretty successful environmentally-friendly garden. There are many local native critters you can delight in should they be attracted to your garden: colorful birds, butterflies, and beneficial insects. On the other hand, you certainly don't want to donate your hard work to the less desirable wildlife.

Try deterrents and physical barriers first: good fencing can usually keep many pests out. Even gophers and moles can't munch through a dug-down flooring of half-inch metal hardware cloth or nibble on bulbs surrounded by wire baskets. Many insects can be washed off plants with a firm stream of water from the hose and netting can often discourage unwanted birds when you've just seeded or plants are fruiting. Always opt for the physical and natural pest controls first. It is easy to just go buy a bottle of chemicals and dump or splash it all over your garden, but poisons can harm the good critters along with the bad ones — and most chemicals that can kill can also be at least somewhat toxic to you, your family, and your pets.

Putting Together the Show (Garden)

If you make regular inspections of your garden, you can catch pest problems early, just like you can find other problems before they become major. You don't have to remove every bad bug that enters your garden. The ones that get through are not likely to do much damage and they can become dinner for the good predators. If things do get out of hand, use commercial insecticides or fungicides carefully and always make sure to follow the instructions on the labels carefully. More often than not, however, if you've designed a garden that is in harmony with where you live, it will balance itself out over time and stay healthy and beautiful with only minor intercession needed. Any garden we build is going to be controlled differently than the way nature would have it, so you will need to keep checking, altering, tweaking, and guiding your garden to keep the show going. Don't be too inflexible. Sometimes you get good surprises, too. There are occasions when a plant self-seeds where it looks great, a rock rolls into a better position than you'd planned, or the tree that was gnawed by an inconsiderate rodent ends up growing back with multi-stems and looks twice as pretty as the original form.

You are both director and audience for your garden show. Create a landscape that will calm your stress, soothe your soul and entice you to *use* it often.

Summary:
The Performance

For some people the perpetual art-in-progress state of a garden provides all the joy they could want. Watching things grow, discovering a flower you forgot you planted come into full bloom, staying fit weeding, digging, and planting, tossing the compost heap — all the myriad jobs in the garden — is a huge reward in itself. Even just cultivating an ornamental container garden on a patio or balcony can feed the soul.

Sharing the garden can also be a thrill. Inviting friends and family to share your garden adds to your audience. Allow your garden to set the mood for entertaining. Let your garden feed you with healthy, fresh fruits, vegetables, and herbs for a fraction of the cost of gas-consuming, shipped-in grocery store foods. Your garden can extend your living space giving you an outdoor room to enjoy when the weather is nice. You can build exercise areas with sport courts, games, swimming pools, child play spaces, or pet areas to keep everyone in the family in good shape. There are so many ways to participate in your own garden show. Most of all, don't forget to take time to enjoy your own masterpiece. Yes, there will always be jobs to do in the garden, but make sure you allow your garden to give back some of the care you put into it.

Plan a space for seating: a bench, a picnic table, or a hammock. Or just throw out a blanket on the ground. Make sure you take a little time to breathe the air being cleansed by the transpiration of the surrounding plant leaves. Drink in the colors and textures. Forget about all the everyday stresses that are waiting at work or in the house. Gardens are therapeutic. Each little plant puts out invisible energies that your mind and body can tune into when you stop all the noise that is running around your head. Take advantage of the healing energy and the relaxing delight offered by your garden in times of demand, like work or family pressures and holidays.

Sometimes even things you enjoy can become stressful. A little time in nature can be like a week in therapy. Let your eyes follow a bug as it trundles on its way to somewhere it finds important. Watch a bird preen as it sits at the top of your favorite tree or shrub. Bend down and examine the kaleidoscopic designs nestling inside the petals of a small flower. Wandering around your garden or sitting in the sounds of nature can sweep out all the dust and cobwebs of nagging thoughts and worries. When you are ready to leave your garden you will likely find yourself feeling as refreshed as if you just finished a cleansing nap or a renewing meditation. People have been doing this for centuries. Rediscovering the huge rewards of being part of your own garden performance can make all the work of creating the show more than worthwhile. Not only have you created an amazing performance of nature with your garden, but you have been a part of it. You will always be a part of nature.

Enjoy the show.

Section Two

INTRODUCING THE CAST

Plant Character Profiles

Since all plants on this planet developed somewhere, even a list of the most popular garden plants would fill a library. The profiles offered here are just random examples of plants that are common or rare, fun or fashionable. You might be surprised in which categories some of these plants pop up. There are plenty more possibilities to choose from to perform in your garden show.

MOISTURE MAVENS
FOREST DWELLERS
MOUNTAINEERS
DENIZENS OF THE DRY
TROPICAL BEAUTIES
PLAINS POPULATION
BEACH BABES
COUNTRY COUSINS
HANDY HERBS

Plants that will strut their stuff in mud, bogs, streams, and even bathe happily in deeper water

MOISTURE MAVENS

ASTILBE

☐ Goat's beard (*Astilbe*)

Photo by Teresa Soule.

Commonly called false goat's beard, with its delicate, cut foliage and feathery blooms in shades of pink, white, purple, and red, it is very decorative and thrives in wet or moist soil in full shade. A hardy plant that does not cower at cold weather, the false goat's beard is naturally found in Europe, North America, Asia, Africa, Australia, and New Zealand. It can grow anywhere from six inches to six feet tall and will appreciate loamy soil.

CYPERUS

☐ Cyperus

A decorative aquatic grass that has been used for crafts and household items for thousands of years, the *Cyperus papyrus* seems to have originated in the Nile Delta area of Egypt. This rhizomatic plant, the paper rush, as it is often called, can grow as tall as sixteen feet and shoots up strong triangular stems topped with a circular cloud that explodes with green-brown flowers and nut-like fruits. The smaller variety, *Cyperus alternifolius*, usually called the umbrella plant, is a native of the swamps of Madagascar. Plants of the *Cyperus* genera are sedges and love moist environments. These two species do not have to actually be grown in water — they will grow well in any soil that doesn't dry out too much. They also prefer warmer temperatures and full sun.

HOUTTUYNIA CORDATA 'CHAMELEON'

☐ Chameleon plant
(*Houttuynia cordata 'Chameleon'*)

Also known just as the chameleon plant or Chinese lizard tail, the *Houttuynia cordata 'Chameleon'* is native to Southeast Asia. This plant has a number of cultivars with ornamental, colorful foliage. It is easily grown in moist to wet, organic soils — so easy that it can become invasive, creeping beyond its boundaries with its rhizomatous roots. Give it sun to part shade and it can form large, thick mats from eight to fifteen inches tall. The variegated cultivars color up best if given full sun.

LOBELIA CARDINALIS

☐ Cardinal plant (*Lobelia cardinalis*)

Photo courtesy of GardenSoft.

The *lobelia cardinalis*, or cardinal flower, evolved in marshes and wetlands from Canada through South America. The brilliant, deep scarlet flowers are adored by hummingbirds and the dark red foliage makes the whole plant very decorative. This showy water plant grows between one and three feet tall in moist but not saturated soil with filtered sun or shade. In hot summer climates, give it more shade and in cold winters it will appreciate the protection of mulch. There are several cultivars available for the garden, all very ornamental.

ZANTEDESCHIA

☐ Calla lily (*Zantedeschia*)

Photo by Teresa Soule.

Though its common name is Calla lily, the *Zantedeschia* is not a lily at all. Growing from a rhizome it braves imperfect conditions by dying back when it becomes too dry or cool for comfort. Growing from eight inches to three feet tall, the calla lily is indigenous to southern Africa where it is happiest growing in the moist marshes. Give this plant shade in hot sun. It will only tolerate light frosts. All parts are poisonous when eaten. There are many species, cultivars, and hybrids offering plants from six inches to several feet in height. The handsome spathe-type blooms come in a wide range of colors. They will grow in moist gardens or as bog plants.

ACORUS GRAMINIUS

- Sweet flag (*Acorus graminius*)

Though called many different things (sweet flag, dwarf sedge, Japanese rush, or Japanese sweet flag), the *Acorus graminius* is a clumping grass with flat, curving blades. It is found naturally in Asia, China, Japan, Korea, India, Thailand, the Philippines, and Myanmar. The cultivar *Acorus graminus 'Ogon'* is also a favorite for garden ponds and boggy areas with its golden variegated foliage. Also popular is the licorice-scented variety. Sweet flag grows between six and eighteen inches high in wet areas with full sun or part shade.

CALTHA PALUSTRIS

- Marsh marigold or kingcup (*Caltha palustris*)

Photo by Barbara Black.

The *Caltha palustris* (marsh marigold or kingcup) is an herbaceous perennial plant of the buttercup family easily recognized by its sunny yellow flowers. Originating in wet, woodland areas in the temperate parts of the Northern Hemisphere, the marsh marigold enjoys light shade. It prefers cooler temperatures and grows in a lush clump up to three feet tall.

GLYCERIA

- Manna grass (*Glyceria*) growing in its native habitat in New England.

Photo by Barbara Black.

Also called mannagrass or sweet grass, *Glyceria* spreads through wet areas with creeping rhizomes. There are species of mannagrass that grow naturally in temperate zones throughout the world, many of which are common to the United States. The variegated form with white-striped leaves is highly decorative for ponds or water gardens. Mannagrass grows up to three feet in bog conditions or in water up to six inches over the top of the soil. Give it sun or partial shade.

JUNCUS EFFUSES

- Common or soft rush (*Juncus effuses*)

A common or soft brush, this is a two to five-foot tall, grassy, bog plant is native to North America, Europe, Asia, Africa, Australia, and New Zealand. A true rush (cylindrical, hollow-stemmed water-lovers) this family offers decorative members that love moist environments. The smaller *Juncus effusus 'Gold Strike'* and *Juncus effusus spiralis* are both ornamental and can grow ten to eighteen inches high in standing or slow moving water. Grow them in either sun or shade.

LOUISIANA HYBRID

- The Louisiana Iris 'Black Gamecock'.

- A field of mixed Louisiana Iris growing in the margins of a water inlet. Photo taken at the Japanese Garden at the Tillman Reclamation Plant, Los Angeles, California.

A water-loving Iris that was derived from interbreeding the bog-types — *Iris nelsonii, Iris brevicaulis, Iris fulva, Iris giganticaerulea,* and *Iris hexagona* — to create a group of very colorful plants that bloom prolifically, these plants are natives of the Southeastern United States. When happy, they will form thick clumps with flowers that stay open only a day, but produce plenty of flowers as they grow into larger clumps.

MYOSOTIS SCORPIOIDES

☐ Water forget-me-not (*Myosotis scorpioides*)

Understandably called the water forget-me-not, the *Myosotis scorpioides* blooms with the small blue flowers characteristic of the land-loving garden favorite forget-me-not, *Myosotis sylvatica*. This water-lover evolved in Europe and Asia, but it has invaded the United States and other areas where it has become naturalized. The plant grows low, usually from four to eighteen inches tall in bogs or high moisture-retaining soil. Give the *Myostis scorpioides* part shade or full sun. In warm climates it can stay evergreen.

PONTEDERIA CORDATA

☐ Pickerelweed (*Pontederia cordata*)

The *Pontederia cordata*, or pickerel weed, grows naturally in ditches, marshes, and other wet areas in the eastern half of the United States and continues to grow as a native down into South America. There is also a community of these plants that may or may not be indigenous to Oregon. It is a decorative plant with bright blue flowers that makes its home along the wet banks of ponds, streams, marshes, and rivers. The pickerelweed grows from one to three feet tall with thick, waxy leaves in full sun. Its leaves are edible. Like too many of the bog plants, the *Pontederia* has been allowed to escape controlled environments and is now an invasive plant in Florida.

SAGITTARIA LATIFOLIA

☐ Arrowhead (*Sagittaria*)

An aquatic plant that gets its common name, arrowhead, from the shape of its leaves, the *Sagittaria latifolia* is also called duck potato, swan potato, tule potato, and wapato (because of its tuberous root). Most species are native to the American continent with a lesser number coming from Europe and Asia. It grows best in bog-like conditions with full or part sun and reaches from eighteen inches to four feet in size. It will tolerate very cold temperatures well below 0 degrees Fahrenheit.

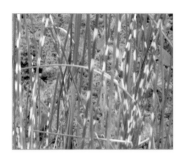

SCIRPUS ZEBRINUS OR SCOENOPLECTUS

☐ Zebra Rush (*Scirpus zebrinus*)

The *Scirpus zebrinus* or *Scoenoplectus* gets its common name, zebra rush, from the hollow, cylindrical grass-like leaves that are striped with white. This bog plant is native to North America. The long leaves double as stems and grow vertically up to four feet high. In the winter the plant dies back and is best cut down so the new growth will display its handsome, clear colors in the spring. Give it sun or part shade.

TYPHA LATIFOLIA

☐ Cattail (*Typha latifolia*). At the end of the season these familiar brown cattails loosen their seeds and almost look like they are exploding

Photo by Barbara Black.

Typha latifolia is the familiar cattail or bullrush. Common to the Northern Hemisphere, it will grow in cold or heat so long as it gets to set its roots into thick, wet mud with or without a layer of water on top. The edible rhizome creeps along creating whole stands of this tall grass. It prefers to bask in full sun. There are tall and dwarf varieties. The tallest can reach ten feet.

EICHHORNIA CRASSIPES

☐ Water Hyacinth
(*Eichhornia crassipes*)

The *Eichhornia crassipes*, or water hyacinth, is one of the best known of the floating water mavens. It grows smooth, green leaves from curious, inflated stems and will bloom in full sun with decorative lilac flowers painted with a touch of blue and yellow. Originally from South America, these plants will not tolerate frost or salt. Like most floaters, they are a source of nourishing food for fish and are efficient at filtering out pollutants from pond water. Also like most surface swimmers they have paddled their way into too many places where they were not invited and are causing local ecological trouble.

MYRIOPHYLLUM AQUATICUM

☐ Parrot feather
(*Myriophyllum aquaticum*)

The *Myriophyllum aquaticum*, or parrot feather, is a plant that prefers to root into soil or mud stretching up to three feet out over the surface of the water. This plant evolved along the Amazon River in South America where pieces can break off and live floating independently or can root when it drifts into a handy location for growing. The delicate ferny green foliage has made it a popular pond plant and, as a result, it has escaped cultivated conditions to become naturalized worldwide, particularly in warmer areas. In some of these areas, like on the West Coast, it is a declared invasive pest.

PISTIA STRATIOTES

☐ Water Lettuce (*Pistia stratiotes*)

The *Pistia stratiotes*, or water lettuce, is a decorative swimmer that dangles long roots under spongy, light-green, ridged foliage. It is ornamental and offers the same useful water filtration qualities as many other floating plants. It also keeps nibbling fish well fed. It, too, has become invasive in some parts of the world. The origins of the water lettuce are unsure, but the oldest records seem to trace back to Africa. This plant is not at all frost-tolerant and shows best in full sun.

AZOLLA PINNATA

☐ Ferny azolla or the mosquito fern (*Azolla pinnata*)

The *Azolla pinnata* (*ferny azolla or the mosquito fern*) is a tiny aquatic fern that has adapted to floating on the surface of slow-moving water. It can form thick mats that will help shade the growth of unwanted algae (*and discourage mosquitoes from finding open water to lay their eggs*) or can be kept as small areas of floating green. In hot sun or cool temperatures, it flushes with a warm, red tint. *Azolla* is highly nutritious for your fish — so nutritious that it is being cultivated to feed chickens and livestock. Africa and Madagascar, India, Southeast Asia, China, and Japan are native homes, but it will thrive in most ponds or water features. Don't let it grow too thickly and stifle the fish in a pond. Instead, scoop out the excess and use it as a wonderful mulch to feed garden areas.

LEMNA MINOR

☐ Duckweed (*Lemna minor*) with young water hyacinths.

Photo by Velvet Heller.

The *Lemna minor*, or duckweed, is a simplified form of plant that floats on or just beneath the surface of the water. The good news is that it is remarkably easy to grow and multiplies fast. It also is an excellent pollutant filter. Duckweed is a high-protein plant that is readily consumed by waterfowl, fish, and is even part of a healthy diet for some people. The *Lemna* family is being studied for its potential food and energy source value for the future. The bad news about Duckweed is that it can easily become invasive and hard to remove if it invades local waterways. It can be introduced easily by sloppy pond care or even be accidentally carried by birds and other animals due to its small size. In ponds it can clog pipes and filters. It originally developed in sunny, slow-moving water in parts of North America, Africa, Asia, and Europe.

MICRANTHEMUM UMBROSUM

☐ Baby tears (*Micranthemum umbrosum*) being appreciated by a frog.

Photo by Genevieve Schmidt.

The *Micranthemum umbrosum*, or baby tears, is a water plant that naturally grows in small ponds and ditches in the southeastern parts of the United States. There are species native to Central America, too. It is becoming very popular for indoor aquaria with its neat carpeting effect. The small plant roots in mud and will spread widely across the surface of the water making a soft, green carpet. Not a plant for cold climates, it will thrive in the sun or shade. Do not confuse this with the land-loving *Soleirolia soleirolii*, another 'baby tears'.

Plant Character Profiles

COLOCASIA ESCULENTA

◻ Taro or the elephant ear (*Colocasia esculenta*)

Colocasia esculenta (*taro or the elephant ear*) is a dramatic plant for a water garden. Indigenous to Polynesia and southeastern Asia, this plant has edible roots used in many traditional Hawaiian dishes and has also been bred to offer cultivars and hybrids with huge, decorative leaves, some blended or splashed with contrasting colors. Most are large-leafed and eye-catching, like the imperial taro or the black taro. Unlike the *Colocasia esculenta*, all parts of these other taros are poisonous. Liking wet, these plants are happiest as bog plants. They flower with the characteristic funnel-shaped, arum-type flower that has what looks like a single petal (*actually an adapted leaf called a bract*) with a tall central rod (*spadix*) on which the tiny true flowers cluster.

GUNNERA TINCTORIA

◻ Chilean rhubarb, dinosaur food (*Gunnera tinctoria*), in bloom.

Photo by Velvet Heller.

The *Gunnera tinctoria* (*Chilean rhubarb or dinosaur food*) grows in southern Chile and Argentina. Its cousin, *Gunnera manicata*, the giant rhubarb, which is also called dinosaur food, comes from Brazil. There is absolutely nothing subtle about these plants. They grow rounded leaves that are two to six feet across on plants that reach eight to twelve feet high. They aren't looking for open water, but do want moist soils. In parts of New Zealand and Ireland, they have made themselves too much at home and are becoming serious invasive pests. They like it warm and moist, so give them full sun and protect them from dry air and cold temperatures. They are unequaled as drama queens in the garden.

LIGULARIA

◻ Spotted leopard plant (*Ligularia aureomaculata* or *Farfugium japonicum aureomaculata*)

◻ Giant leopard plant (*Ligularia tussilaginea 'Gigantea'* or *Farfugium japonicum 'Gigantea'*)

Ligularia, or the leopard plant, has a large number of species mostly distributed throughout the Himalayas, Japan, Taiwan, and China. Three favorites often used in landscaping are the *Ligularia dentata*, *Ligularia stenocephala*, and *Ligularia tussilaginea 'Gigantea'* (*giant leopard plant*). These are large plants with dramatic round or triangular, sometimes tooth-edged leaves. The *Ligularia* blooms with flat or tall spires of yellow or orange flowers. Some varieties are only about one to three feet high whereas others can stretch to six, spreading wide and making a bold statement in the garden. Give them part sun to shade and copy their native habitat of streamside and damp meadows with deep, fertile soil if you want to keep them happy. Beware, slugs and snails love *Ligularias*.

NELUMBO NUCIFERA

◻ Lotus (*Nelumbo nucifera*) in its native environment.

Photo by Diane Sullivan.

The *Nelumbo nucifera*, or lotus, is a stately plant that grows in the shallow, quiet water found in ponds and marshes. Common to Asia, Australia, New Guinea, and the Middle East, this plant is the source of many romantic tales and is the flower of the Sacred Lotus. The lotus has an edible root used in Asian cuisine. Offering huge rounded leaves and enormous flowers usually in pinks, whites, magentas, or yellows, these plants can grow from two to fifteen feet tall. They make bold statements in the water garden and need full sun to strut their stuff.

NYMPHAEA

◻ Water lilies (*Nymphaea*)

The *Nymphaea* encompasses more than fifty species of water lilies to decorate the water garden. There are even more choices with all of the hybrids that have been developed to offer a wide range of flower colors and even colored or patterned leaves. These plants have evolved in aquatic environments all over the world and are most commonly divided into 'hardy' varieties and the more cold-sensitive 'tropical' water lilies. All grow from creeping rootstocks that anchor the plants two to six feet deep in the muddy bottom of slow-moving water. These are heavy-feeding plants and need at least six hours of sun to bloom well.

Plants adapted to woodland conditions; these are the growers that evolved in a world of trees, moisture, and interdependency on their neighbors. Their repertoire is likely to show them off best in gardens with rich or organic soils, a fair amount of rainfall, and often a bit of sheltering shade.

FOREST DWELLERS

6

Plant Character Profiles

Ground-Huggers and Climbers
These are woodland residents with a low profile.

CONVALLARIA MAJALIS

☐ Lily of the valley (*Convallaria majalis*)

Photo by Teresa Soule.

The *Convallaria majalis*, or lily of the valley, is native to the cooler, woodland parts of the Western Hemisphere on the East Coast of America, in parts of Asia, and Europe. The lily of the valley usually grows from six to ten inches tall and blooms with little nodding white or pink bells. Give it shade and medium water. It prefers cool to heat and is a hardy little plant that goes dormant in winter. It can become invasive.

CLEMATIS

☐ Clematis

Clematis has different common names for various species and hybrids — traveler's joy, virgin's bower, old man's beard, leather flower, or vase vine — but mostly it is simply known by its Latin name, *Clematis*. Most of these vining plants have extremely showy flowers and evolved in the temperate zones of the Northern Hemisphere with very few being native to the tropics. These are limestone-lovers so don't give them acid soil. They are also particular about where they are planted, insisting on having roots firmly planted in the shade and flowering head smiling in the sunshine. All parts of the plant can cause skin irritation and are toxic if eaten. Some clematis vines can clamber up to twenty feet in height.

HEDERA HELIX

☐ English or common ivy (*Hedera helix*)

The *Hedera helix* (*English or common ivy*) is a creeping and climbing plant. It has been known to clamber up to 100 feet, grabbing walls or tree trunks with tenacious little roots. It is an energetic ground-cover that will blanket horizontal or vertical surfaces in both cold and warm climates. English ivy is still a favorite in many gardens and as a potted house plant despite the fact it has been declared a noxious, invasive plant in a number of states across the country. The decorative, classic effect it has when growing on brick or stucco walls makes it a favorite for gardens. However, you should think twice before introducing it into your environment. It could take over — and it makes a good shelter for unwanted rodents and snakes.

LAMINUM MACULATUM

☐ Deadnettle (*Lamium maculatum*)

Photo by Barbara Black.

Also referred to as deadnettle, spotted deadnettle, or purple dragon, this plant grows from four to eighteen inches tall in woodlands and grasslands with fertile soil that doesn't dry out. There is a wide choice of ornamental cultivars with small, spotted, blotched, or patterned leaves that will form a cheerful carpet in part or full shade. Leaves can be green, white, silver, yellow, or patterned with a mix of these colors. Flowers are usually pink, white, or lavender-pink, but deadnettle is usually grown more for its foliage than its flowers. It survives frosty temperatures, but only remains evergreen in warmer climates.

LONICERA SEMPERVIRENS MAGNIFICA

☐ Coral honeysuckle (*Lonicera sempervirens magnifica*)

The *Lonicera sempervirens magnifica*, or coral honeysuckle, is a native honeysuckle common to the eastern half of the United States. This one has startling red flowers with orange interiors and grows to about twelve feet in well-drained, average soil with sun to light shade. Like honeysuckles from all over the world, the flowers are a favorite of hummingbirds and lots of birds love the berries. It is a non-invasive plant unlike many other honeysuckle vines like *L. japonica*, *L. maackii*, *L. morrowii*, and *L. tatarica*. There are many varieties of honeysuckle that grow as bushes or as vines and offer flowers in a wide range of colors and fragrances. Most prefer the woodland setting, but there are those that have evolved in mountainous and plains areas and also a few species that are adapted to dry areas with hot sun.

PACHYSANDRA PROCUMBENS

- Allegheny *spurge* (*Pachysandra procumbens*)

Photo by Jane Milliman.

- *Japanese Spurge (Pachysandra terminalis) is the more commonly grown, but more invasive Pachysandra.*

Photo by Katie Elzer-Peters.

The *Pachysandra procumbens* also goes by the name of Allegheny spurge or Allegheny pachysandra. This *pachysandra* is a native species that resembles the highly invasive Japanese pachysandra, but originally grew up in the deep, organic soils of the woods in Southeastern United States. It rarely grows over a foot in height and blooms with scented white flowers. This is an easy-maintenance ground-cover that can handle cold winter temperatures, but will do better with a little protection. It will be happiest with light shade and rich soil. The *Pachysandra terminalis* is not a native of America, though it is a plant that also prefers a moist, slightly acid soil like its American cousin. The *Pachysandra terminalis* is called the Japanese spurge and is native to Japan and China. It is a more popular garden plant, but has become an invasive pest in parts of the United States.

SCHIZOPHRAGMA

- Climbing hydrangea (*Schizophragma*) at the Weston Nursery, Hopkinton, Massachusetts.

Photo by Barbara Black.

The *Schizophragma*, or climbing hydrangea, is a shade-lover that can grow up to heights of thirty feet in ideal conditions. It likes a rich, moist soil. This big, hardy vine is natural to the forests of China and Japan. It will fill a large space with its lush foliage and typical hydrangea-type flowers in clusters of white or blushed pink.

TRACHELOSPERMUM JASMINOIDES

- Confederate jasmine (*Trachelospermum jasminoides*)

The *Trachelospermum jasminoides*, or confederate jasmine, grows naturally in parts of Asia, Korea, China, Vietnam, and Japan. This wonderfully scented, flowering, woody climber will twine up trees to great heights or sprawl over ground and fences in the home garden. It will grow in woodlands and fields preferring stands of tress for clambering up as a natural support. Give it part shade and average water.

VINCA MINOR

- Periwinkle (*Vinca minor*)

The Vinca minor, or periwinkle, evolved in the woodlands and forests of Europe, northwestern Africa, and central and southwestern Asia. This is a rambling vine that will grow from six to eighteen inches high, but can creep five or six feet horizontally. It is effective for covering slopes, open areas, or tumbling over walls or down the side of pots. The periwinkle handles hot weather better with a little shade and can be planted as an annual in places where it will succumb to hard frosts. You can find an assortment of cultivars with varying leaf forms and different colors of blue and purple flowers.

VIOLA

- Violet (*Viola*)

Photo by Diane Sullivan.

The *Viola* is a large genus in the violet family that includes the charming little woodland violets that like it moist and shady and the meadow violets common to higher elevations like the Johnny-jump-up (*the original parent to hundreds of colorful annual pansies that brighten gardens all over the world*). Although these plants are primarily indigenous to the temperate climates of the Northern Hemisphere, there are violet species found in the mountains of the Andes, Hawaii, and Australasia. The violet is the state flower of four states: Rhode Island, Illinois, New Jersey, and Wisconsin. Small growers from four inches to under a foot tall, native plants bloom in yellows, purples, blues, white, bicolors, and tricolors. Most of these violets are short-lived perennials (*often grown as annuals*) and thrive in cooler summer temperatures. Meadow-growers like the bedding pansies can handle full sun.

ACER PALMATUM

▫ Japanese maple or smooth Japanese maple *(Acer palmatum)*

The *Acer palmatum (Japanese maple or smooth Japanese maple)* is a tree that can grow from a small dwarf of only a few feet high to a larger specimen of thirty feet. Foliage can be cut or split into fingers or fine, feathery divisions. This woody plant originated in Asia in parts of Japan, North and South Korea, southeastern Russia, and areas of China and Mongolia. Japanese maples are decorative plants that have been cultivated for ornate foliage and handsome leaf color. Handling both heat and cold, the biggest climate enemy of the Japanese maple seems to be dry, desiccating winds or direct, hot sun that can burn their delicate foliage. The most sun-tolerant varieties tend to have less finely cut foliage. Give them average water, a bit of humidity, and slightly acidic, rich soil with good drainage.

CORNUS FLORIDA

▫ Flowering dogwood
   (Cornus florida)

Photo by Barbara Black.

This well-known flowering dogwood is native to the eastern half of the North American continent with species into Texas and south into eastern Mexico. A hardy, small growing, ornamental tree that loses its leaves in the winter (*deciduous*), the *cornus florida* blooms with easily identifiable pink or white four-petal bracts that look like flower petals even though the real flowers nestle inconspicuously in what looks like the center of the bloom. There is a wide choice of cultivars and hybrids to decorate the garden. Trees usually reach between fifteen to thirty feet tall and the majority of hybrids do best with morning sun and afternoon shade although most can handle either sun or shade depending on where you live. Give them a moist, acidic soil. They can brave very cold temperatures.

SYRINGA

▫ Lilac *(Syringa)*

The *Syringa*, or garden lilac, is a member of the olive family that evolved in southeastern Europe and eastern Asia where it happily makes its home in cool, temperate woodland and scrubland environments. Because of the beautiful flowers and their delightful perfume, there have been many hybrids developed from the double-flowered French lilacs to the *Descanso* hybrids that allow lilacs to be grown successfully in warmer climates. Give these plants sun or part shade, plenty of moisture, and soil that is more on the alkaline side. The *Syringa vulgaris (common lilac)* can grow up to fifteen feet usually on multi-stemmed trunks whereas some of the dwarf cultivars will stay to five or six feet high. The Chinese tree lilac — the *Syringa pekinensis* and *Syringa reticulata* — and the Japanese tree lilac will grow from twenty to forty feet tall.

TAXUS CUSPIDATA

▫ Spreading yew or Japanese yew
   (Taxus cuspidata)

Photo by Barbara Black.

The *Taxus cuspidata (spreading yew or Japanese yew)* is native to Asia in China, Korea, and Japan as well as the far southeastern parts of Russia. This is a handsome evergreen conifer that grows from a few feet to fifty feet in full sun or part shade. There are many cultivars and hybrids. Give it regular water and plant it where it has room to spread. It will look at home in a woodland garden in either cold or hot climates.

TSUGA CANADENSIS

▫ Canadian or Eastern hemlock
   (Tsuga canadensis)

Photo by Barbara Black.

The *Tsuga canadensis (Canadian or Eastern hemlock)* adds a forested look to the garden. Give it lots of space to grow since this fir tree will grow between forty and seventy feet high in the garden. In its natural habitat of eastern North America, there are lofty specimens that have soared to over 150 feet in height. This handsome evergreen is the state tree of Pennsylvania. It can handle both cold and heat so long as it gets plenty of moisture in the soil. When young, it should be planted in part shade to full shade the same as it would grow in its woodland home. A tough tree, the Canadian hemlock will handle cold winters and warm summers — just make sure it has plenty of room to grow.

TUBEROUS BEGONIA

□ Tuberous Begonia

Photo by Teresa Soule.

A favorite houseplant all around the world that hails from South America and southern Africa; these colorful plants can grow twelve to eighteen inches tall and need moist humus. There are so many cultivars and hybrids that these plants can grow with single or double flowers in a multitude of colors. They can spill over hanging pots or mound up in warm climate gardens. The tuberous begonia needs light shade, warm temperatures, and is not fond of too much heat or high humidity.

DAFFODIL AND NARCISSUS

□ Commonly the larger-flowered plant of the Narcissus genus are referred to as 'Daffodils' whereas smaller flowers like this paperwhite are often termed 'Narcissus'.

"Daffodil" and "Narcissus" are names often used interchangeably for the many species, cultivars, and hybrids of this popular flower. Native to Western Europe, Asia, and North Africa, these are true bulbs. There are many different varieties of narcissus and hybrids that offer colors in cream, pink, yellow, white, and apricot; they are sometimes decorated with orange or green. You can find plants that grow from six to twenty inches tall. Tolerant of a wide range of soils, these bulbs like open woodland areas or gardens in full sun. They tolerate heat or cold, but most flower better with some cold to help initiate buds. Like all bulbs, let the foliage turn yellow and die down before removing it so energy can be stored for next year's growth. Daffodil bulbs are poisonous and rarely eaten by animal pests. Bulbs are also toxic to humans and domesticated pets.

Plant Character Profiles

AQUILEGIA

◻ Columbine (*Aquilegia*)

The *Aquilegia*, or columbine, is a meadow and woodland plant often growing at higher altitudes all around the world in the Northern Hemisphere. Most of the columbine species have adapted to higher mountain conditions with a smaller stature and have developed lusher foliage and larger flowers in the gentler environment of the moist woodlands. Garden hybrids have been developed with a broad range of sizes, colors, single or double flowers, and characteristic spurred petals that are either emphasized or underemphasized for interesting shapes and forms. Native columbines grace North America, Britain, and much of Europe as well as happily populating many gardens with lovely cultivars and hybrids. Versatile plants, columbines will take sun or shade, cold or heat, and a wide range of soils so long as they drain well.

AZALEA

◻ Azalea

The *Azalea* is a popular plant that evolved in the wooded environments of Asia, Europe, and North America. A large number of native *Azalea* species naturally developed in the southeast of the United States. *Azaleas* are lovers of moisture-retaining, acidic soils. They thrive in shade and can bloom happily where many other plants would gasp for more light. The thousands of cultivars offer cold hardy plants from one feet to larger shrubs at six feet high. Colors range through reds, oranges, yellows (*the yellow actually being Rhododendron luteum*), pinks, purples, and whites with pink spots. Favorite garden shrubs, these forest growers are willing to handle mild sun or even a residency in pots.

BRUNFELSIA PAUCIFLORA

◻ Yesterday-today-and-tomorrow-plant (*Brunfelsia pauciflora*)

Photo by Velvet Heller.

The *Brunfelsia pauciflora* sports the long common name of yesterday-today-and-tomorrow-plant. This unique flowering shrub starts blooming with deep blue flowers that fade to lavender on the second day and bleach white on the third, which accounts for the common name. All colors are displayed on the plant at the same time making the shrub a very colorful conversation piece in the garden. The *Brunfelsia pauciflora* evolved in the woodlands of Brazil. Plants grow to between three and six feet tall with a similar spread. Although they prefer temperatures above fifty degrees Fahrenheit, they will brave the occasional light frost. The berries should not be eaten as they are toxic.

CAMELLIA

◻ Camellia

The *Camellia* is a favorite garden plant. *Camellias* are evergreen shrubs and trees native to eastern and southern Asia. With a wide range of species, cultivars, and hybrids, these are mostly adapted to organic, moisture-retaining, acidic soils common to woodland areas. Some ornamental species like the *Camellia sasanqua* are tolerant of full sun, but most prefer a little more shade; although in climates where the sun is not too intense, most do fine without a lot of extra shading. Although there are heat and cold resistant varieties, the majority of *Camellias* like temperatures above freezing and below ninety degrees Fahrenheit. These are not good choices for lime soils or dry areas.

COTONEASTER

◻ Cotoneaster (*Cotoneaster 'Coral Bells'*)

Photo by Velvet Heller.

The *Cotoneaster* is indigenous to temperate areas of Asia, Europe, and northern Africa. Sizes range from creeping ground-covers to fifteen-foot shrubs. The lower varieties have adapted to the high elevations, many in the high peaks of

China, whereas larger shrubs inhabit open areas in woodlands and scrublands. Most of the popular garden *Cotoneaster* hybrids developed for their *corymbs* (*a flattened group of tightly branched flowers*) in white, pink, and occasionally reddish flowers, and their ornamental bright red-orange clusters of berries. There are many cultivars for the garden, though some have now become invasive in parts of Europe, New Zealand, Australia, and California.

DICENTRA SPECTABILIS

▢ Bleeding heart or Dutchman's breeches (*Dicentra spectabilis*)

Photo by Teresa Soule.

The *Dicentra spectabilis* (*bleeding heart or Dutchman's breeches*) is indigenous to the woodlands in North America from British Columbia to California. Give the bleeding heart typical woodland conditions of part shade to full shade with a soil rich in compost that will hold moisture. Plants can grow to about three feet in height and handle cold or warmth.

DIGITALIS PURPUREA

▢ Common foxglove (*Digitalis purpurea*)

The *Digitalis purpurea* (*common foxglove*) is a shade-loving plant from Europe and the Iberian Peninsula where it grows in rocky crevices, woodlands, pastures, and hillsides. There are many cultivars and hybrids offering colorful, tiered flowers in white, purple, pink, and yellow hues. The plant is poisonous, though it has been prepared and used medically for centuries to treat heart conditions. This ornamental plant does best with some shade, a slightly acid loam, and regular water. The *Digitalis purpurea* is a biennial (*grows the first year and then flowers, sets seed, and dies the second*), but there are a number of decorative foxgloves that are longer living perennials. Frost-hardy, the common foxglove will grow from three to six feet tall when in bloom.

FUSCHIA

▢ Fuchsia

Photo by Velvet Heller.

Fuchsia is one of those plants that uses its Latin name as a common name. *Fuchsias* grow as small trees and shrubs. Most developed in South America, but there are also species from Central America and New Zealand. Sizes of these plants can vary from six inches to six feet in height for garden plants although there are larger, tree-type species that are less commonly grown in the garden. Famous for their dangling flowers — sometimes dressed with bell-like skirts in contrasting colors — *Fuchsias* bloom in reds, pinks, whites, magentas, and purples. Most are frost intolerant and prefer gentle sun, part shade, or full shade with a rich, moist soil. *Fuchsias* are good plants for container gardening.

HEUCHERA

▢ Alum root or coral bells (*Heuchera*) now come in a variety of leaf colors and forms with sprays of red, pink or white flowers.

The *Heuchera* (*alum root or coral bells*) evolved in woodlands, hills, and rocky cliffs across North America with more species growing on the western half of the country than the eastern. There are hundreds of colorful hybrids with leaves of amber, lime green, chartreuse, deep purple, and more; some have patterns in the foliage. Delicate sprays of white, pink, or coral flowers are also ornamental. Many of the hybrids with highly colored or patterned foliage do better with some shade and a richer soil, having been bred from more of the woodland slope natives of the East. The tougher cultivars and hybrids that like more sun, fast drainage, and less water often are bred from the Arizona native *Heuchera americana*. The alum roots range from small alpine varieties of only a few inches tall to about three feet for the biggest California growers.

HOSTA

▫ Hostas in the garden.

Photo by Barbara Black.

The *Hosta* is native to northeast Asia, mostly China and Japan, with some more recent species from Korea. Popular garden hybrids abound offering an assortment of foliage colors and designs with stalks of blue, purple-pink, or white flowers; some are more showy than others. In their native habitats, most *hostas* get more rain than many parts of the United States, so they won't mind if you give them plenty of water. The soil should echo forested soils with plenty of organic material incorporated that will drain well yet stay moist. Shade or dappled shade will also help recreate the umbrella of sun protection that will keep them thriving. Plant sizes vary from six inches to three feet tall with leaf size and shape variations. *Hostas* are very cold-hardy.

KALMIA LATIFOLIA

▫ Mountain laurel (*Kalmia latifolia*)

Photo by Barbara Black.

Best known as the mountain laurel, the *Kalmia latifolia* is a showy shrub native to the eastern half of the United States; this Kalmia is also related to blueberries, azaleas, and rhododendrons and, like these other plants, it requires a moisture-retaining, acid soil rich in organic matter just like in its native forest habitat. Preferring some shade, it will handle full sun if kept moist and humid. The Mountain Laurel grows from eight to twenty feet in height and is often wider than tall.

PIERIS

▫ Forest flame (*Pieris*)

The *Pieris* is often called forest flame, Andromeda, or fetterbush. This forest native evolved in the mountainous regions of North America, southern parts of Asia, and the island of Cuba. Foliage tends to start red before fading to green. There are many cultivars that range in height from two to eighteen feet. White flowers are sometimes flushed pink or green and hang decoratively in multiple strands like dangling charms on a chain. This is a shade-lover that grows well on acid soil; give it plenty of water in the garden.

PULMONARIA

▫ Lungwort (*Pulmonaria*)

Photo by Teresa Soule.

The *Pulmonaria* has a whole string of common names: lungwort, soldiers and sailors, spotted dog, Joseph and Mary, Jerusalem cowslip, and Bethlehem sage. These are popular garden plants as most cultivars stay under two feet in height. There is a wide selection of cultivars and hybrids with leaves that are often spotted, flushed, edged, or patterned with colors. Add blue or purple (*occasionally red, pink, or white*) flowers and you have a plant that is hard to resist in the woodland garden. Native to deciduous forests in Europe, Western Asia, and a single variety in Asia, the lungwort likes it shady with plenty of moisture.

RHODODENDRON

▫ Rhododendron

Photo by Teresa Soule.

The *Rhododendron* is another of those plants that uses its Latin name as a common name. There are more than eight hundred species and many more hybrids to choose from for the garden. The *Rhododendron* is natural to temperate climates found in North America, Asia, and Europe as well as tropical parts of Australia and southeastern Asia. These shrubs can be small ground-covers or 100-foot trees and grow from coasts through high mountains. Although *Rhododendrons* have a very wide range of habitats, all like rich, well-drained soil high in acid, and plenty of rain. They do best in climates that are not extreme in heat or cold. There are many cultivars and hybrids that will add a wide range of bright, clustered open-bell flowers that are showy in the garden.

Known as the alpine growers, these are the best performers for well-drained, rocky, high-altitude gardens. They will show off nicely in rock gardens. Some of these high-elevation plants have developed specialized skills to cope with the wet from melting snow or thin air conditions.

MOUNTAINEERS

6

Plant Character Profiles

King of the Mountain
With respect for its venerable age and history, this tree gets the category all to itself.

PINUS LONGAEVA

◻ Bristlecone pine (*Pinus longaeva*) proving that plants can survive even harsh environments.

The *Pinus longaeva* is the amazing bristlecone pine tree. It can be planted in the garden as a very slow-growing pine. This tree has bragging rights to being the oldest tree species in the world. There are trees still alive that are almost 5,000 years old. The bristlecone pine is native to high elevations of mountains in six western states of the United States with the oldest specimens in the California White Mountains. It grows in lean, alkaline, rocky soils. The bristlecone pine can grow to sixty feet, but in its native habitat it rarely reaches anywhere near that height. It grows in extreme, exposed conditions on hungry, rocky, high calcium soils. In the garden, it will grow in more ideal conditions, but still so slowly that you won't live to see it soar to any great height. Do not give it rich soil or anything other than excellent drainage. If you want to see these ancient living relics at their best, the most impressive stand can be found in the Bristlecone Pine Forest in the White Mountains of California.

AJUGA REPTANS

▫ Bugleweed (*Ajuga reptans*)

The *Ajuga reptans* is a handsome ground-cover plant with an assortment of common names: blue bugle, bugleweed, common bugle, carpetweed, carpet bugleweed, or burgundy lace. Whatever you call it, this plant originated in Europe and there are some very colorful hybrids that offer bronze, purple, or green leaves sometimes spattered or streaked with pink, lavender, or white. Flowers are small spires of deep blue. The plants only grow three to six inches tall and like gentle sunshine, part shade, or full shade with regular garden soil and ordinary water.

ANDROSACE

▫ Rock Jasmine (*Androsace*)

Photo by Mary Kirtland.

The *Androsace*, or Rock Jasmine, is a small plant only a couple of inches in height that forms cushions of green studded with pink or white flowers. An alpine native from arctic regions in central Asia like the Himalayas and the mountains of southern and central Europe including the Alps and the Pyrenees, give them cool temperatures. They can take full sun, but need to be planted in sandy, gritty peat or loam with excellent drainage. In their native habitat, the rock jasmines love to grow deep roots between stone fissures. They are sweetly scented when in bloom. Charming little plants, these are the top choices for the rock garden where they can be seen up-close.

ARABIS

▫ Alpine rockcress (*Arabis*)

Photo by Teresa Soule.

Arabis is known as the mountain or alpine rockcress. It evolved on the slopes of southern Europe and northern Africa as well as in parts of Asia, North America, and a few spots in the British Isles. This is a small plant no higher than a foot tall with white to dark pink flowers. Plant it in a garden with good drainage and low to regular water. Give it full to part sun and cool temperatures to keep it happy.

CAMPANULA CARPATICA

▫ Carpathian harebells (*Campanula carpatica*)

Photo courtesy of GardenSoft.

The *Campanula carpatica* is a plant known as the *Carpathian harebells* or *tussock bellflower*. This flower stays small at six to twelve inches high and offers decorative white or blue, bell-shaped flowers. It is native to the Carpathian Mountains in Eastern Europe where it can handle sun or part shade and plenty of moisture that drains freely. A favorite cultivar is "Blue Chips."

DIANTHUS

▫ Dianthus

The *Dianthus* is a group of plants that includes carnations, Sweet Williams, and pinks. Most of these plants are native to parts of Asia and Europe with some odd numbers in northern Africa and one in arctic areas of the North American continent. A large number of *Dianthus* plants grow in higher elevations and most prefer slightly sweet (*alkaline*) soil. There are hundreds of well-behaved cultivars and hybrids available for the garden, painted in reds, pinks, creams, yellows, whites, and purples, some fringed or double flowered. Give them good drainage. The majority of the *Dianthus* garden selections are likely to grow from four inches to a foot in height, but some species can grow from two inches to three feet. This is one plant that will reward you richly by continually re-blooming if you keep dead flowers removed (*deadheading*). Cultivars for the garden are often biennial and will bloom in their second year before they die. If happy they can reseed themselves. There are also perennials that will come back year after year.

LEONTOPODIUM ALPINUM

- Edelweiss (*Leontopodium alpinum*)

Photo by Kylee Baumle.

The *Leontopodium alpinum* (edelweiss) is probably one of the most famous of the alpine plants. Endeared to all with its own song from the musical *The Sound of Music*, this small plant has leaves covered in a white down that makes it look as if it were made of felt. It grows from four to fifteen inches in height and likes locations where temperatures don't get too hot. A native daisy, the edelweiss grows in poor, limestone soils usually in elevations higher than 6,000 feet in the mountains of Europe and Asia. It is also found in some parts of South America where it is thought to be native. Like so many alpine plants, it loves fast-draining soils, cool or even cold temperatures, and plenty of sunshine. The blossoms will be a little creamier colored in partial shade.

LEWISIA

- Lewisia tweedy

The *Lewisia* species are all indigenous to the western parts of North America. The showiest species are *Lewisia cotyledon* and *Lewisia tweedyi*; the most ornamental garden hybrids often have been bred from these two species. Flowers show off in pinks, whites, corals, and peaches, and often offer striped or blended petal colors. Leaves form a low rosette (*circular or spiral growth*) and plants usually stay under six inches in height even when in bloom. Give them sun or part shade and excellent drainage. They can take cold temperatures and are likely to go dormant in the warmth of summer.

SEDUM

- This mixed groundcover of sedums creates a living patchwork quilt. Photo taken at the Castaic Water Agency — Conservatory Garden and Learning Center, Santa Clarita, California.

- Stonecrop (*Sedum kamtschaticum*)

The *Sedum*, or stonecrop, is a low-growing plant common to the Northern Hemisphere. These plants are succulents, meaning that they have adapted to store water in their leaves so they can handle drought and fast-draining soil. Different species of stonecrop vary in their needs. The majority of stonecrops stay under a foot in height and there are plenty that grow less than six inches. Species that have evolved in high altitudes like the *Sedum anacampseros* or *Sedum obtusatum* are very cold tolerant. Stonecrops are drought-tolerant and thrive in full sun or part shade in rocky soils. The 'Sedum' now goes by the name "Hylotelphium."

SEMPERVIVUM

- Houseleek or hen and chicks (*Sempervivm tectorum*)

Photo courtesy of GardenSoft.

- You can see the "hen and chicks" concept for this Sempervivum hybrid when looking at the young offsets of this plant.

Photo by Teresa Soule.

The *Sempervivum* (*houseleek or hen and chick*) is an ornamental little plant that tends to grow in ground-hugging clumps with interesting forms and shapes as well as spikes of attractive flowers. They, too, are succulents and are native to mountainous regions in a number of places throughout Europe, the Mediterranean, and the Old World. The *Sempervivum* grows well on and between rocks in mountain, alpine, and sub-alpine areas. Their ability to store water in their thick leaves allows them to live on sunny rocks and in stony places. They have evolved in high elevations so they can handle very cold temperatures. In hot sun they will need shade or part shade.

Artistic Alpines

Most of these make fine garden plants that will show off with a creative flair so long as you cast them in the appropriate roles.

ACONITUM

▫ Monkshood (*Aconitum columbianum*) in its native mountain environment.

Photo by Diane Sullivan.

The *Aconitum* (*monkshood*) is a decorative plant that grows in higher altitude meadows, often in mountainous terrain where the soil remains damp yet drains fast. *Aconitum napellus* (*the common monkshood*) is a species frequently planted in the garden for its mysterious, deep blue flowers. The yellow-flowered *Aconitum lycoctonum* (*alpine wolfsbane*) is found in the Alps of Switzerland and the *Aconitum columbianum* (*western monkshood*) is a wildflower native to the slopes on the western side of the Americas. These plants prefer shade and are very showy in the garden. Plant these where there is no chance of little children or pets mouthing them since they are highly toxic if ingested. Monkshood is native to many areas in North America, Europe, China, and several other areas. The common thread between all the monkshoods is their liking of moist, mountainous territories — and the fact they are all poisonous. They grow best in the cooler summer climates.

ALSTROMARIA

▫ Lily of the Incas (*Alstromaria*)

The *Alstromaria*, or lily of the Incas, grows from small tubers. This decorative bloomer has a number of hybrids that offer many color combinations with painted blends, stripes, and spots. Grow them in the garden for their beauty or for pulling stems of flowers to create indoor arrangements. (*Plants do better with flowering stems removed from the base with a quick tug rather than cut with a tool.*) The lily of the Incas prefers reasonably warm temperatures like in its native habitat at altitudes of 1,500

to 2,000 feet in the mountains of Peru and Bolivia. Give it well-drained soil and full sun or dappled shade. It can sulk when transplanted. Some people can experience skin allergies from contact with the plant, so be careful when picking the flowers.

CALAMAGROSTIS BRACHYTRICHON

▫ Reed Grass or Korean feather reed grass (*Calamagrostis brachytrichon*)

The *Calamagrostis brachytrichon* (*reed grass, Korean feather reed grass*) is native to the mountain regions of East Asia. This is a handsome ornamental grass with slightly pinkish flower plumes that are decorative in the garden. It grows in a clump of about two feet tall, but doubles its height when in bloom. Its favorite native haunts are in the higher elevations with moist, rich soil, but it is adaptable in the garden. This ornamental grass is happy in mild sun or shade. It grows in cool or warm temperatures.

GENTIANA

▫ Gentian (*Gentiana andrewsii*)

Photo by R. Lutz.

The *Gentiana* is a very large genus of mostly blue or white flowered plants known as gentian. An inhabitant of mountainous regions in temperate America, Asia, and Europe with additional species in Africa, New Zealand, and Australia, gentians can be fussy about growing conditions. Gentians insist on very well-drained soil that is on the acid side with ample organic material. They resent having their roots disturbed. The gentians offered for sale for home gardens are the easiest to grow. Give them full sun or part shade and cool to cold temperatures. They are perfect for the temperate rock garden.

GYSOPHILA PANICULATA

▫ Baby's breath (*Gypsophila paniculata*)

Photo courtesy of GardenSoft.

The *Gypsophila paniculata* is a favorite for cut flower arrangements with roses. It is known as baby's breath because of its delicate panicles of tiny white or sometimes pink flowers. Naturally growing in the dry steppes of Eastern Europe it is comfortable with gravelly, dry conditions in rock and limestone. As a result, it is fond of calcareous soils and, in fact, the name "gypsophila" actually means "chalk-loving." Give this plant a well-drained environment with regular water, plenty of sand and stone, avoid acid soils, and let it bask in sunshine. Most varieties stay under three feet. Don't be fooled by its delicate-looking flower stems. It has become an invasive plant around the Great Lakes region. High humidity climates are not very successful with the *Gypsophila paniculata*.

PYRANCANTHA

- Firethorn (*Pyracantha*)

The *Pyracantha*, or firethorn, naturally ranges from Southeast Europe through Southeast Asia with many species indigenous to China, often found in hills and mountainous areas. Heights range from four to twenty feet. Thorny, woody stems bloom with masses of white flowers that turn into many red, orange, or yellow berries that are technically pomes — the name for fruits of the rose family. (*Although the firethorn looks nothing like the common rose, it is in the same family.*) A drought-tolerant plant that likes good drainage, the firethorn likes plenty of sun and makes a good plant for a wildlife garden since it offers food and habitat to many types of birds and other wildlife. It is a hardy shrub that accepts a broad range of soil types. The *Pyracantha angustifolia* has become invasive in some areas so you may want to try a species like the *Pyracantha coccinea* instead.

SAXIFRAGA

- Rockfoil (*Saxifraga*) in the garden.

Photo by Teresa Soule.

- Rockfoil (*Saxifraga bronchialis*) close-up.

Photo by Lisa Bourey.

Often called rock foil, rock-breaker, or saxifrage, there are more than 480 known species of the *Saxifraga*, with the majority making their homes in alpine environments. Most are small-growing, successful ground-covers, mostly evolving in sub-arctic climates in the Northern Hemisphere. Some grow as tall as a couple of feet high. They make excellent choices for rock gardens, areas of natural scree, and cold climate gardens. They naturally grow in clefts of rocks where the foliage hunkers down low and sends up delicate sprays of mainly white, pink, yellow, or red flowers. They do not like extreme heat or dry. Some choice cultivars are the tufted saxifrage (*Saxifraga caespitosa*), mossy saxifrage 'Purple Robe' (*Saxifraga x arendsii*), and Saxifraga 'Peter Pan'.

SCABIOSA

- Pincushion flower (*Scabiosa*)

The *Scabiosa* is one of the many species of *Scabiosa*, a decorative flowering plant known as the pincushion flower. Native to Europe and Asia these plants have acclimated to different elevations and conditions, usually preferring the higher locations. Many cultivars are crosses with the *Scabiosa columbaria* and *Scabiosa atropurpurea*. Hybrids have provided a whole range of garden flowers that come most commonly in pinks, blues, and purples. There are also some species in white and pale yellow, with new hybrids in maroon. Some are tiny ground-huggers whereas others can grow to two feet with big, showy flowers. All prefer a well-drained loam with plenty of sun, but they are forgiving of a wide range of less than ideal conditions.

SILENE DIOICA

- Red campion (*Silene dioica*) growing naturally.

Photo by Diane Sullivan.

The *Silene dioica*, or red campion, is a small, bright-pink, flowering plant endemic to rocky slopes and wooded areas in diverse regions throughout Europe. In the garden, give the red campion sun to partial shade and moist, neutral, or alkaline soil. There are handsome hybrids that will stay below two feet in height.

XEROPHYLLUM TENAX

- Bear Grass (*Xerophyllum tenax*)

Photo courtesy of Forestfarm.

The *Xerophyllum tenax* goes by one of many common names: bear grass, squaw grass, soap grass, quip-quip, and Indian basket grass. Although the foliage looks like an ornamental grass, this plant is part of the lily family. Bear grass is native to meadows and open forests in the higher elevations of western North America. This is a white-flowered plant that grows up to five feet tall. It grows as a fire-follower — gaining stronger, new growth after wildfires. Give it cool to cold temperatures, excellent drainage, and rocky soil in full sun. It is a tough grower that will do well in a garden with natural arctic conditions.

*Mountain environments are perfect for the development of bulbous type plants,
which hide in their little storage homes beneath the soil until the conditions are
just right for them to make a flamboyant appearance.*

CROCUS

❑ Crocus

Photo by Teresa Soule.

Crocus are colorful little flowers that grow from corms. They are native to coasts and woodlands from the mountainous regions of the Old World and into Asia as far as the western parts of China. Although these cheerful little plants are tough enough to endure most soils, freezing temperatures, and variable moisture, they prefer sunshine and good drainage; they are less happy in dry or hot conditions. Being so versatile, they could easily have gone into my 'Country Cousins' group, but since they do so well in alpine gardens where choices are more limited, I decided to list them under the Mountaineers.

GALANTHUS NIVALIS

❑ Snowdrop (*Galanthus nivalis*)

Photo by Teresa Soule.

The *Galanthus nivalis* is probably the most common garden species of the small bulbous flower called snowdrop. Some of the first bulbs to bloom in the late winter, these natives from the European continent can cover the ground with their white flowers when they grow in masses. They like some shade and rich, moisture-retentive soil with good drainage; growing only about four inches tall, they're ideal for the cool temperature garden, rock garden, or alpine garden.

Here are some of the showy plants native to hot, dry areas that can help create a beautiful, drought-resistant landscape. They brave baking sun, lean soils, and periods of low rainfall.

DENIZENS OF THE DRY

ACACIA REDOLENS

▢ Acacia redolens 'Low Boy'

The *Acacia redolens 'Low Boy'* or *'Desert Carpet'* are both prostrate forms of the Acacia. These are popular Australian native plants that grow two to three feet tall and can spread as wide as twelve feet. They are an excellent choice as ground-cover for a large, hilly area where there is summer dry, poor soil, and low humidity. *Acacia redolens* can take winter temperatures as low as 15 to 20 degrees Fahrenheit as well as the full, hot sun in the summer.

DYMONDIA

▢ Silver carpet (*Dymondia*)

The *Dymondia* (*silver carpet or carpet gazania*) is a remarkably low-growing plant. It spreads out roughly two feet wide although the plants will only grow about two inches high. A perfect ground-cover for hot, dry areas, this native of the South African coastal plains has green leaves with white-silver undersides and blooms with yellow daisy flowers. It is ideal for lawn replacement or for filling in between pavers and flagstones. You can also use it in any area where a dense, flat mat of drought-tolerant greenery is needed. Give the *Dymondia* full sun, hot summers, low water, and even ocean salt spray. It will accept winter cold down to 20 degrees Fahrenheit.

IBERIS SEMPERVIRENS

▢ Candytuft (*Iberis sempervirens*)

The *Iberis sempervirens*, or perennial candytuft, is a small, evergreen plant that can look like a miniature shrub in a formal garden or it can spread as a rich green mat in a less formal design. It is a handsome, low-growing shrub when not in bloom, but explodes into life when it smothers itself with icy-white flowers. A neat-growing plant, the candytuft will grow from eight inches to two feet tall. It originated in the Mediterranean area so it won't take more than light frost. Give it sun or some light shade, and shear it down when flowers fade or it becomes lanky. Go light on water: this is a good drought-resistant plant.

MYOPORUM PARVIFOLIUM

▢ Creeping myoporum (*Myoporum parvifolium*)

The *Myoporum parvifolium* goes by the common names of creeping myoporum, creeping boobialla, slender myoporum, and dwarf native myrtle. It is a mat-forming, low ground-cover that originated in Australia. Although it usually grows only six to twelve inches high, it can spread from three to eight feet in diameter. Flowers are small and white. A tough plant that is ideal for covering slopes and open areas of fast-draining soils, the *Myoporum* is an attractive evergreen plant that takes full, hot sun or part shade. It will survive the occasional drop of temperature to the low 20s. There are several named cultivars.

Tough Trees & Large Shrubs
These big guys are experts in water conservation and come equipped with a well-adapted root system for seeking it out.

ARBUTUS UNIDO

□ Strawberry tree close up of bloom.

□ Strawberry tree (*Arbutus unido*)

Photos by Velvet Heller.

The *Arbutus unido*, or strawberry tree, is an ornamental evergreen tree that evolved in Western Europe, the Mediterranean, and Ireland, where the Gulf Stream warms the coastal air. These are small trees from six to thirty feet tall. The shorter sizes can be found with *Arbutus unido compacta*. Trees can be grown with single trunks or multi-stemmed. This is a drought-tolerant tree that prefers full sun and soil with lime. It will handle some frost, but not cold winters.

ARCTOSTAPHYLOS

□ Manzanita (*Arctostaphylos*)

The *Arctostaphylos*, or manzanita, is an evergreen shrub or small tree characteristically found in the well-drained, hot, dry summer climate of the chaparral on the West Coast of the United States and central Mexico. The smooth, red wood is ornamental, tough, and often used in bird perches because it can withstand sharp claws and beaks. Plants can grow close along the

ground or reach up to twenty feet. Both berries and flowers are edible. Use these plants for their decorative arches of small white and pink, dangling, lantern-like flowers, colorful berries, and handsome growth habits in areas where temperature ranges are wide, soils are poor, and heat can soar in the summertime.

BANKSIA

□ Banksia

Photo by Diane Sullivan.

The *Banksia* is one of those Australian plants that range from ground-covers and shrubs to medium-sized trees. More subtle in color than some of the more flamboyant Proteas (*see tropical plants*) but equally dramatic in shape and form, *Banksias* can offer decorative shaped foliage and bizarre but ornamental flowers that are often compared to pine cones or bottle brushes. The best Banks to grow in hot, dry, sunny regions are the hairpin banksia (*Banksia spinulosa*), Hinchinbrook banksia (*Banksia plagiocarpa*), coast banksia (*Banksia integrifolia*), 'Giant Candles' (*Banksia 'Giant Candles'*), Cape York banksia (*Banksia dentata*), and *Banksia petiolaris*. Most of these plants are somewhat frost shy, but the coast banksia will take cold down to around 20 degrees.

BUDDLEJA DAVIDII

□ Butterfly bush (*Buddleja davidii*)

Photo by Velvet Heller.

The *Buddleja davidii*, often spelled "Buddleia davidii," is one of the *Buddleja* species commonly referred to as the butterfly bush — and it really does attract birds and butterflies with its long, flower-studded conical tails of tiny florets that come in blues, purples, pinks, and whites (*with other species offering yellows and even oranges*). Native to the drier parts of the United States, south to Chile, Africa, and warmer parts of Asia and Central China, this is a versatile, large-growing shrub that has become invasive in parts of the Untied Kingdom. Plant breeders have developed smaller varieties that grow only two to three feet like the 'Flutterby'™, 'Lo & Behold'™, and 'Blue Chip'™ cultivars. Other butterfly bushes can reach five to twelve feet. They like full sun, well-drained soil, and are highly ornamental.

CORDYLINE AUSTRALIS

◻ Cabbage tree (*Cordyline australis*)

The *Cordyline australis*, or cabbage tree, is a New Zealand native. This attractive plant starts out looking grass-like with stiff basal leaves and then grows a tall trunk before branching and becoming tree-like and stretching up to sixty feet tall (*although it usually stays considerably smaller in the garden*). Give this dry denizen soil that drains freely and plenty of warm sunshine. Although the cabbage tree became popular in landscapes as recently as the 1990s, many hybrids have subsequently been developed to decorate the garden. Cultivars offer colored foliage in deep reds, rusts, yellows, and even hot pinks. This New Zealand plant likes very different conditions from its tropical cousin *Cordyline fruticosa* (*see tropical beauties*).

NERIUM OLEANDER

◻ Oleander (*Nerium oleander*)

The *Nerium olcander*, or oleander, is a flowering evergreen shrub that grows up to twenty feet tall with a few dwarf hybrids that grow as low as four feet. The oleander has ornamental single or double flowers mostly in reds, whites, pinks, pale yellows, and salmon tints, usually sweetly scented. It likes good drainage and is tolerant of a wide range of soils, accepting hot summer temperatures and taking some frost in the winter. A very resilient and decorative plant, its biggest drawback is that it is highly poisonous to both humans and animals if ingested. The oleander has been cultivated so widely that its origin is unsure, although Asia is thought to be its native homeland.

OLEA EUROPEA

◻ Venerable old olive trees (*Olea europea*)

Photo by Diane Sullivan.

The *Olea europea* is the olive tree that graces the Mediterranean and other warm, dry summer climates. Producers of the edible olive, these trees are lovely shade trees that grow into craggy and sometimes twisted forms. Tough and tolerant, you can find varieties like 'Majestic Beauty', 'Wilsonii', 'Fruitless,' and 'Swan Hill'® that have insignificant fruits or are completely fruitless for landscaping use where the fruit can become a nuisance or where pollen can cause allergies. Olive trees like plenty of sun and fast-draining soils. They can suffer damage under 20 degrees Fahrenheit.

The *Parkinsonia* and *Cercidium* are two excellent desert trees that thrive in strong, hot sun. Both flower with very decorative sprays of yellow flowers and grow from twenty to thirty feet tall. Both can sometimes develop an attractive weeping habit of growth.

PARKINSONIA ACULEATA

◻ One of the Palo Verdes: the Mexican Palo Verde (*Parkinsonia aculeata*).

The *Parkinsonia aculeata* is called the Mexican palo verde, Jerusalem thorn, or jellybean tree. It is one of four Parkinsonias native to Southwest United States, down through Mexico, and South America, to northern Argentina. It is easily identified by its long, wispy leaves and its prominent thorns. It is the most cold tolerant of the *palo verdes*, surviving temperatures just under 20 degrees Fahrenheit.

CERCIDIUM FLORIDUM

◻ Another colorful Palo Verde: the Blue Palo Verde (*Cercidium floridum*). Photo taken at the Theodore Payne Foundation for Wildflowers and Native Plants, Sun Valley, California.

The *Cercidium floridum*, or blue palo verde, is another sun-loving, water-wise tree. It has feathery foliage and is native to the desert areas of Arizona and California. It needs a little more warmth than the *Parkinsonia*, not tolerating more than the lightest frost. Both palo verdes are easily identifiable by their green bark — adaptations to desert living by minimizing leaf surface and using bark for photosynthesis.

Plant Character Profiles

PUNICA GRANATUM

☐ Pomegranate (*Punica granatum*)

Punica granatum, the edible and decorative pomegranate, is native to Iran, southern Europe, and northern India. The pomegranate is a large shrub or a small tree with showy red flowers that pollinate into the big, red, seedy fruit familiar at the grocery store. There are hybrid pomegranates that have been developed to produce little or no fruit in exchange for large double or single white, red, pink, or bicolor flowers. There is also a *Punica granatum 'nana'* variety that grows dwarf to only a few feet in height. Give these plants full sun and low to moderate water. The full-sized pomegranate usually grows no larger than fifteen feet making it a handy size for most gardens.

SCHINUS MOLLE

☐ California pepper tree (*Schinus molle*)

Schinus molle, the California pepper tree (*and sometimes the more accurately named Peruvian pepper tree*), isn't from California at all, although that may be hard to believe once you see how many of them are being grown in the state. Native to dry areas of South America and Mexico, these decorative trees are ideal for full sun, fast-draining soil, and plenty of summer heat. The decorative berries are edible and are sold as 'pink peppercorns,' although they are not related to the usual culinary pepper. California peppers are good, drought-resistant, evergreen trees. They make handsome shade trees that will grow to roughly fifty feet tall. Like some plants that like their new homes a little too well, the *Schinus molle* has become invasive in some parts of the United States.

YUCCA

☐ Yucca (*Yucca whipplei*) at home in the California chaparral.

The *Yucca* is a sculptural plant that evolved in the arid or semi-arid areas of North and Central America. These plants are likely to be found making their home in deserts and badlands, rocky hills and mountains, sparse woodlands, chaparral, prairies, open grasslands, and even in sandy areas of the coast. They have adapted to handle high heat and frosty cold. Tough plants, yuccas add vertical elements and contrast in the garden and are ideal for landscapes where conditions are demanding. They prefer full sun, but tolerate some shade and need little water. Yuccas look like clumps of sword-like foliage when young and usually grow single trunks as they rise into sparse-looking, small trees from six to twenty-two feet tall. Most varieties can handle at least light frost.

SCILLA PERUVIANA

☐ Peruvian lily (*Scilla peruviana*)

The *Scilla peruviana* is confusingly known as the Peruvian lily, hyacinth of Peru, Cuban lily, and Portuguese squill with only the last name being accurate. This is a showy flower that grows six inches to a foot high from a large bulb and is native to Portugal, Italy, and Spain. The introduction of 'Peru' came from the name of the ship on which the plant was first imported. This highly decorative bulb blooms with strikingly bright blue flowers. White flowers are also available. It grows in late winter, blooms in early spring, and goes dormant all summer and autumn. Give it full sun, temperatures that don't fall below 5 degrees, lean soil, and good drainage.

DICHELOSTEMMA

☐ Blue dicks, purplehead, or brodiaea (*Dichelostemma capitatum*)

The *Dichelostemma* is a plant that grows from small corms in the western United States and northern Mexico. The *Dichelostemma capitatum*, also known as the *Dichelostemma pulchellum*, goes by the common name of blue dicks, purplehead, or brodiaea. The *Dichelostemma capitatum* is tolerant of a variety of soils and conditions from low coastlines through open valleys and woodlands to scrubland up to about 8,000 feet. Adapted to full sun or light shade, the height can be variable from six inches to two feet tall. They go dormant in summer heat and survive all but hard frosts. The *Dichelostemma* needs excellent drainage. These plants tolerate poor soils and will grow well after wildfires as the corms survive the fast-moving heat and take advantage of a lack of competition in the burn-cleared land. Plant these showy blue flowers in a designed garden or naturalize them in wildflower gardens.

ACHILLEA MILLEFOLIUM

▫ Yarrow (*Achillea millefolium*)

The *Achillea millefolium* is a yarrow that is native to the western parts of North America, yet can be found all over North America. In fact, many varieties grow naturally all over the world. The *Achillea millefolium* has a rather wild look and is usually seen with small, flat platters of small white flowers. There are also more colorful cultivars for the garden like a millefolium 'Paprika', 'Fire King', 'Apricot Delight', 'Red Beauty', and 'Cerise Queen'. Yarrows of this group can grow a little rangy, but some varieties are neater than others. They rarely reach more than two feet tall so you can also use them as ground-cover plants in sun or part shade.

BERLANDIERA LYRATA

▫ Chocolate flower (*Berlandiera lyrata*)

The *Berlandiera lyrata* earns its common name "chocolate flower" as it is a night-blooming flower that will stay open into the morning hours to show off its subtly designed, yellow, daisy flowers that fill the air with a luscious chocolaty scent. Tough, small, and tolerant of very lean soils, the chocolate flower grows about six to eight inches tall. This plant evolved in the dry patches of well-drained soil throughout the West of the United States and in Mexico in full sun. The chocolate flower will survive cold into the low teens.

Caesalpinias are very showy flowering plants from warm climates.

CAESALPINIA PULCHERRIMA

▫ One Caesalpinia is known as the Peacock flower (*Caesalpinia pulcherrima*).

Photo by Diane Sullivan.

The *Caesalpinia pulcherrima* is a shrub that has brilliant red and orange frilly flowers in big clusters. Also called Barbados pride or the peacock flower, it is thought to be native to the West Indies and will grow nicely on well-drained, poor soils. Depending on where it grows it can reach from four to twelve feet in height. Not reliably frost-hardy, give it full sun.

CAESALPINIA GILLIESII

▫ Another showy Caesalpinia is the Desert bird of paradise (*Caesalpinia gilliesii*).

The *Caesalpinia gilliesii* (*desert bird of paradise or 'Mal de Ojo'*) is also very showy in flower. This Caesalpinia blooms with huge clusters of big yellow, flared, trumpets blaring out long, bright red anthers; it is native to Argentina and Uruguay and has naturalized in parts of Texas. Growing from nine to twelve feet tall the desert bird of paradise will put on a brilliant show in the garden even with very little summer water, dry air, and baking, hot sun. It seems to tolerate temperatures into the low 20's. There are several other ornamental Caesalpinia species that are also drought-resistant in the garden.

CASSIA NEMOPHILA

▫ Desert cassia (*Cassia nemophila*)

The *Cassia (Senna) nemophila* (*desert cassia*) is an Australian native that will add beauty to the dry, lean soils and hot summer sun of gardens in the chaparral or desert communities. The desert cassia is a favorite for attracting butterflies and it offers a stunning display of early springtime yellow flowers. It grows to about six feet tall and survives temperatures down to 20 degrees. Historically, the Cassia was one of the principal plants of the Holy Anointing oil used to anoint priests and kings in the Middle East during ancient times. It is a genus that offers showy shrubs and trees that have been used for their medicinal properties, most blooming in shades of yellows or whites. One non native South American Cassia, *Senna pendula var. glabrata*, also known as the climbing cassia, is considered an invasive plant in Florida. The Cassia has evolved in a number of different areas around the world and has both desirable performers and undesirable varieties for the garden — so pick and choose carefully.

CISTUS

☐ Rock rose (*Cistus*)

The *Cistus*, or rock rose, can grow as a neat shrub that gets smothered with white or pink flowers in early spring. It can also sprawl or look gangly depending on how it is grown. This is an evergreen plant that grows from two to five feet in height depending on the cultivar. The deep green foliage looks handsome year-round. The rock rose is native to the temperate regions of Europe, some areas in North and South America, and the Mediterranean. This plant evolved in poor soil areas where wildfires are not rare and has adapted to surviving fast-moving fires better than most other ordinary plants. Give it winter water and lots of sunshine. It will take some frost, but not very cold winters.

ERIOGONIUM

☐ Conejo Buckwheat is a colorful but endangered plant (*Eriogonium crocatum*).

The *Eriogonium* offers a wide selection of plants generally called buckwheat. Most have a sprawling or mounding habit of growth usually from one to three feet high. These small shrubs bloom with tight clusters of small flowers in white, pink, rose, yellow, and even chartreuse. Some varieties are decorative after blooming as the seed heads turn bright rust red. Plants can have hard, green foliage or soft grey-white leaves. Most are very decorative, accepting of lean, hungry soils, and are highly drought-tolerant. They are also quite flammable in wildfires. Buckwheat plants grow wild in places all over North America except in the Northeast. They are a major food source for native butterflies and moths. These plants are useful for ground-cover plantings on slopes and open, dry areas in full sun. Cold tolerance varies with different buckwheat varieties.

ESCHSCHOLZIA CALIFORNICA

☐ California poppy (*Eschscholzia californica*)

The *Eschscholzia californica*, or California poppy, is a low-growing, showy plant native to the West of the United States. Wild plants grow from six inches to two feet and flower in hot shades of orange or yellow-orange tints. Cultivars now come with silky or fluted petals and bloom in reds, pinks, and whites as well as warm orange and yellow shades. These are short-lived perennials as they are often planted for a single year. Give them full sun and low water.

EURYOPS

☐ Bush daisy or African bush daisy (*Euryops*)

The *Euryops* (*bush daisy or African bush daisy*) is found naturally in central and southern Africa. It is a woody plant that grows into a shapely shrub about two to four feet tall. Covered with ornamental, large, bright yellow daisies, the bush daisy blooms in mid to late winter when there are few plants flowering in the garden. The *Euryops chrysanthemoides* is a handsome shrub with deep green foliage whereas the *Euryops pectinatus* is clothed in a softer gray-green foliage. Both like fast-draining soil and will do well in full or partial sun. There are several cultivars available. The bush daisy is not reliably frost-hardy.

FREMONTODENDRON

☐ Flannel bush (*Fremontodendron*)

The *Fremontodendron* is also known as the flannel bush. The fuzzy leaves are decorative and felt-like. Some people can find them irritating to the skin. Plants are studded with yellow-orange single-petal flowers. Most varieties grow to large shrubs, but there is a smaller variety, *Fremontadendron californicum decumbens*, that grows to a more demure height of four feet. This is a dry-summer California native that can take dappled shade or full, hot sun. It likes really poor, fast-draining soils. Because it is shallow rooted, plant the flannel bush where there is some protection from high winds. Cold-hardiness varies with location, but it will usually take temperatures into the 20s.

LAVENDULA STOECHES

- Spanish lavender
  (*Lavendula stoeches*)

The *Lavendula stoeches*, or Spanish lavender, is from the Mediterranean region and areas in North Africa. Growing from eighteen inches to two feet tall and equally wide, this is probably the most cold tolerant of the lavenders. It will handle temperatures that fall into the mid or even low 20s. A lovely, scented plant that likes dry, warm summers but will also handle some humidity, there are a number of hybrid cultivars that flower in purples, blues, pinks, whites, and greens as well as combinations of colors. Grow it with plenty of sunshine in lean soil with low water.

OENOTHERA

- Mexican primrose or pink lady
  (*Oenothera speciosa*)

The *Oenothera* has a number of species that usually fall under the common names of native primroses or sundrops. These open-faced, pink, yellow, or white flowering plants are native to the mountains and deserts of the Americas where they can grow from six inches to almost ten feet in height depending on the species. The most common Oenothera used in the home garden is the *Oenothera speciosa* with common names of pink lady, pink evening primrose, showy evening primrose, or Mexican primrose. These wildflowers are native to the lower half of the United States and into Mexico. They become downright invasive in a garden with well-drained soil and full sun. Give them hot summer temperatures. They'll survive some frost in the winter since they'll die down to the ground.

PENSTEMONS

- Scarlet Bugler (*Penstemon centranthifolius*)

The *Penstemon eatonii* (firecracker) and *Penstemon centranthefolia* (scarlet bugler) are two red-flowered California native plants that are perfectly at home in intense desert and chaparral conditions. There are hundreds of penstemons that grow across the world in diverse climates. These two are ideal for tough, sun-baked, dry conditions, yet add fiery color to the garden. These red Penstemons range from one to two feet tall and can form large clumps that can look like small decorative shrubs. They tolerate some frost. Look for Penstemons of all colors for the garden. Since there are species adapted to cold, hot, dry, and moist climates, there's likely to be a good selection of flowers for your garden no matter where you live. Some of the garden hybids boast spikes of big flowers in eye-catching colors.

PHLOMIS FRUTICOSA

- Jerusalem sage (*Phlomis fruticosa*)

The *Phlomis fruticosa*, or Jerusalem sage, is a handsome plant that is not, in fact, a sage (*Salvia*) at all. Jerusalem sages are native to the Mediterranean, China, and Asia and flower in yellow, pink, purple, and white. All are loved by moths and butterflies. The *Phlomis fruticosa* sports yellow flowers and grows in an attractive clump to about three feet in height. There is a shorter variety, the *Phlomis lanata*. Both these plants like the full, hot sun and fast-draining, lean soils. Other Phlomis species can grow as tall as five feet and offer up whorls of pink or lilac-pink fuzzy flowers similar to the yellow varieties. Many of these are native to Albania, Cyprus, Greece, Italy, Turkey, and regions of the former Yugoslavia now known as the State Union of Serbia and Montenegro. Most Phlomis will also tolerate partial shade and some frost.

ROMNEYA COULTERI

- Matilija poppy (*Romneya coulteri*)
- Matilija poppy flower close-up

The *Romneya coulteri*, or Matilija poppy, is another California native. Growing five to six feet tall, the Matilija poppy spreads by underground runners into large stands. The light green leaves look fresh and bright especially against dark colors. The huge white crepe-paper flower petals show off big, butter-yellow centers. The large size of these plants and flowers make a bold statement in the garden. They can be fussy about where they like to grow, but when they are happy they can be equally hard to get rid of. Give them full sun or part shade, poor, fast-draining soil, and avoid root disturbance. The Matilija poppy is frost hardy to just under 20 degrees.

SISYRINCHIUM BELLUM

□ Western blue-eyed-grass
(*Sisyrinchium bellum*)

The *Sisyrinchium bellum* is the Western blue-eyed grass that is native to areas west of the Sierras like California and Oregon. With its small stature and grass-like foliage, use the western blue-eyed grass as a ground-cover, a flowering accent, an ornamental grass garden, or a low, delicate-looking foil for shrubs or plants with a mounding habit of growth. Plants look good grouped or singly and grow from eight inches to a foot in height. Give blue-eyed grass full sun or lightly dappled shade and good drainage. It handles hot sun and some frost.

TRICOSTEMA LANATUM

□ Wooly blue curls (*Tricostema lanatum*)

The *Tricostema lanatum*, or wooly blue curls, is a remarkably showy shrub when in bloom. It covers itself with long spikes of fuzzy blue and purple flowers with long, whisker-like anthers. Wooley blue curls is a woody California native shrub that can grow to about four feet tall and sprawl six feet wide. It needs exceptionally good drainage and no water whatsoever during summer months. Unless you have perfect chaparral conditions in hot summer sun with poor, gravelly soil, don't try to grow it. It is very fussy. However, if you do manage to get this plant to thrive in your garden, you will have a star performer to make your neighbors jealous.

TEUCRIUM FRUTICANS

□ Bush germander (*Teucrium fruticans azureum*)

The *Teucrium fruticans* is a bush germander that will grow from three to five feet tall and of a similar width. The *Teucrium fruticans azureum* has soft grey foliage that looks bluish when the shrub becomes smothered with its sky blue flowers in late winter. This hardy germander will add its unusual but welcome color to the drought-resistant garden when there is little else in bloom. It is native to Northern Africa. It is also resistant to nibbling deer. Give it plenty of sun and average to poor soil.

Plants in this category are the showy performers from either warm, sultry climates that create a garden reminiscent of an island paradise or are tougher than they look but create the same luxurious appearance.

TROPICAL BEAUTIES

Glamorous Grass-like Growers

These are not true grasses, but have flat-bladed leaves that offers a vertical, grass-like effect. Most grow slowly, stems elongating into trunks that eventually turn them into small trees.

DRACAENA

- Dracaena marginata tricolor is a colorful dragon tree often grown indoors.

The *Dracaena*, or Dragon tree, is native to Africa with several species from southern Asia and a single one from Central America. There are two main types of dragon tree: one group that grows in the arid semi-desert and desert areas and the more shrubby, delicate dracaenas grown in tropical gardens and as house plants. The tropical plants tend to have thinner stems and less stiff leaves. Both grow to small trees, up to twenty or thirty feet tall, in their native habitat. An example of the desert Dracaena is the *Dracaena draco* that is hardy to the low twenties. It will take hot sun or light shade and is drought tolerant. A familiar tropical Dracaena is the *Dracaena marginata*, the red margined houseplant that likes shade, rich soil, warm temperatures, and average water. Many varieties and hybrids of the dragon tree sport showy, colorful leaves, especially those from the tropics. Tropical varieties prefer high humidity and warmth all year round.

CORDYLINE FRUTICOSA

- Ti plant (*Cordyline fruticosa*)

The *Cordyline fruticosa* has a number of common names: cabbage palm, good luck plant, palm lily, ti plant, and the Hawaiian ki. Although many people think of this plant as being from Hawaii, it is naturally found in tropical Southeast Asia, parts of Melanesia, and Australia as well as New Guinea and parts of Polynesia. Some hybrids boast brilliantly colored leaves and because of their decorative looks they are often grown as house plants. In their homelands and in tropical gardens these plants can grow tree-like to twelve feet tall. There are a number of cultivars available from these flashy-colored plants. They like part or full shade, rich soil, humidity, and plenty of well-drained water. You will also notice this plant has a cousin, the *Cordyline australis*, that grows in Australia and is one of the dry denizens. These are just two of the roughly fifteen species of Cordyline.

PANDANUS VEITCHII

- Screw pine (*Pandanus veitchii*) full grown specimen.

Photo by Katie Elzer-Peters.

- The variegated or white-striped, dwarf Pandanus (*Pandanus baptistii*) can be grown as a house plant.

Photo by Barbara Black.

The *Pandanus veitchii*, or screw pine, is endemic to the Old World tropics and the South Sea Islands of western tropical Africa. This is a tree-like plant with propeller like leaves. It produces edible fruit and nuts, but some people can suffer skin irritation when handling the plant. This is another of the truly tropical plants that needs warm temperatures, plenty of well-drained moisture, and humidity. It can grow on tropical shores with salt-tolerant roots and will reach heights of between ten and thirty feet. Growing in sun or shade, the screw pine shows no tolerance for cold. There is a more ornamental white-striped dwarf, Pandanus (*Pandanus baptistii*), native of New Britain Island off of New Guinea, that likes similar conditions, but makes a fine potted plant indoors in bright light.

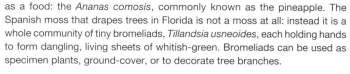

as a food: the *Ananas comosis*, commonly known as the pineapple. The Spanish moss that drapes trees in Florida is not a moss at all: instead it is a whole community of tiny bromeliads, *Tillandsia usneoides*, each holding hands to form dangling, living sheets of whitish-green. Bromeliads can be used as specimen plants, ground-cover, or to decorate tree branches.

Bromeliads grow from just an inch or two big to ten feet tall. Most can't handle much frost, but there are some that can survive temperatures down to 10 degrees. Many grow bright, unusual flowering bracts and flowers that almost look as if they were fabricated with brilliant, man-made colors. They are showy enough to make splendid focal points in the garden or conversation pieces as houseplants.

Only a few terrestrial bromeliads like full sun. The majority evolved in tropical jungles as understory plants with the protecting branches sheltering them overhead.

BROMELIADS

- Spanish moss drapes like a stylish shawl on this tree (*Tillandsia usneoides*).

Photo by Diane Sullivan.

- Native epiphytic bromeliads.

Photo by Diane Sullivan.

- The remarkably-colored blue Puya or Sapphire Tower Puya (*Puya alpestris*) in bloom at the *Mildred E. Mathias Botanical Garden at the University of California Los Angeles.*

- A garden full of colorful bromeliads at the Ganna Walska Lotusland, Montecito, California.

The *Bromeliads* are decorative, tropical plants that grow in the form of a rosette (*a circular shape in which leaves grow from a central point like the petals of a rose*). *Bromeliads* all evolved in the Americas, mostly from Central and South America, but there are some from the United States. One exception is the *Pitcairnia Feliciana*, which makes its home in West Africa. *Bromeliads* are either terrestrial (*grow on the ground*) or epiphytic (*grow perched on trees or other aerial footings*). One is grown commercially

SOLEIROLIA SOLEIROLII

- Baby tears (*Soleirolia soleirolii*)

The *Soleirolia soleirolii* has an impressive collection of common names like baby tears, angel tears, mind-your-own-business, peace-in-the-home, mother of tears, and more. It is a bright green spreading plant that originated in the northern Mediterranean area; mostly in Italy and the island of Corsica. Creating a ground-hugging carpet of soft, bright green, tiny, round-leaf foliage, baby tears blooms with miniature white flowers. It grows lush with higher humidity. As a soft ground-cover, it forms neat mats only about an inch high, but can mound up to five inches. Keep it moist and offer it part to full shade. Baby tears doesn't like temperatures that dip below 45 degrees. Although it looks like an inviting green carpet, it doesn't handle much foot traffic.

TRADESCANTIA VIRGINIANA X ANDERSONIANA 'SWEET KATE'

- Sweet Kate spiderwort (*Tradescantia virginiana x andersoniana 'Sweet Kate'*)

The *Tradescantia virginiana x andersoniana 'Sweet Kate'*, or Sweet Kate spiderwort, is not a tropical plant, but it is a fine choice for creating a tropical-looking garden where conditions are not ideal for heat and humidity-lovers. A spreading plant, this spiderwort creeps along the ground, mounding up to eighteen inches in height. It is a hybrid derived from wild spiderworts native to eastern North America. Give it sun or shade and moist to regular soil. It will go dormant in cold winters, but will survive to under 0 degrees. The deep blue, three-petal flowers are set off by chartreuse foliage creating an unusual color effect ideal to create the illusion of an exotic plant fit for the tropics.

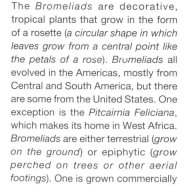

Taller Tropicals

These are plants to fill a larger area with lush growth. Unless noted, don't expect any of these tropicals to withstand frosty temperatures.

BRUGMANSIA

◻ Angel's trumpet (*Brugmansia*)

The Brugmansia, or angel's trumpet, is a large shrub or small tree that originated in South America and decorates itself with three to seven inch flaring flowers in white, pink, cream, yellow, apricot — and one cultivar with red — dangling trumpets. These woody plants can grow from six to thirty feet tall. The flamboyant angel's trumpet likes moist but well-drained humus and shows off in the sun or shade. It is a frost shy plant, but in warm climates is a show-stopper when in bloom. The flowers are perfumed, particularly in the evening, but all parts of the plant are poisonous.

FICUS BENJAMINA

◻ Weeping fig (*Ficus benjamina*)

The *Ficus benjamina* (*weeping fig, Benjamin's fig, or just ficus tree*) grows well in warm environments like its native homes of Australia and the southern parts of Asia. This ficus tree is the official tree of Bangkok, Thailand — a sure sign it likes a tropical climate — and is popular in gardens in the mildest parts of the United States. Even a light frost will burn its foliage. Accepting sun and part or full shade, the *Ficus benjamina* will grow to forty feet in most gardens although it can grow close to one hundred feet in ideal native conditions. Give it normal to low water and good soil. It is adaptable to pot culture indoors or out. Ficus is a large genus with many decorative trees, shrubs, and vines that are mostly inhabitants of tropical climates.

HELICONIA

◻ Lobster claw (*Heliconia*)

Photo by Diane Sullivan.

The *Heliconia* is one of those plants that embodies the look of tropical glamour. It grows large, dangling lobster-like claws of colorful bracts (*adapted leaves*) that look like they're made of ornamental plastic. Some of the bracts are thick and waxy while others are more slender and bird-like. The smaller, colorful flowers pop out of the showy bracts. Give lobster claw plants plenty of humidity, warmth, and a rich, loamy soil. You'll find Heliconias growing in tropical Asia or Hawaii. They'll need the same conditions in the garden or grow them in the controlled environment of a greenhouse. There are smaller and larger Heliconias; the tallest can reach up to thirty feet in height. There are also plenty of varieties that will make a handsome, colorful backdrop for your tropical garden show at five to twelve feet.

HIBISCUS

◻ China rose (*Hibiscus rosa-sinensus*)

Photo by Diane Sullivan.

The *Hibiscus* is a large group of flowering plants. There are many lovely garden plants that are part of the mallow family, members of which grow in a wide range of habitats all over the world. Most commonly people think of the tropical varieties like the huge open flowers of the Hawaiian-type flowers when talking about the Hibiscus. These plants are not native to Hawaii, but rather to tropical East Asia. The *Hibiscus rosa-sinensus* (*China rose*) has been bred to flower in a wide range of colors with small to huge flowers, single and double, clear colors and blends. These are showy tropical plants that grow in size from dwarf shrubs of only a couple of feet tall to small trees. Give them most, rich soil and sunshine or part shade. You can even grow them indoors in large pots with excellent light.

MONSTERA DELICIOSA

▢ Swiss cheese plant (*Monstera deliciosa*)

Photo taken from the Mildred E. Mathias Botanical Garden at UCLA, California.

The *Monstera deliciosa* is the dramatic plant known as the Swiss cheese plant. This imposing plant can climb up to sixty feet, grabbing tree trunks all the way up with its grappling air roots. These plants grow huge split leaves with natural holes set decoratively in the leaves. The Swiss cheese plant will rarely reach these sizes when grown as houseplants or in most cultivated gardens. Native to tropical rainforests in the Americas, these climbers produce edible fruits (*which is where the 'deliciosa' comes from*). Grow them where they have strong supports to climb and where temperatures stay warm with plenty of humidity. Rich, moisture-retentive soils will please them. Due to its tolerance for low light, this is another tropical plant that has been adapted for indoor container growth.

MUSA AND ENSETE

▢ Banana (*Musa*) in bloom and fruit.

Photo Diane Sullivan.

The *Musa* and *Ensete* are two different generas that house the banana plants we know and love as traditional images of the tropics. A few bananas are edible; most are grown for their decorative qualities. Natural to tropical Africa and southeastern Asia, they thrive in a tropical environment of moisture-filled air and damp soils that are rich in humus. Don't try growing the edible bananas *Musa acuminata* or *Musa balbisiana* in your garden unless you live in a warm, moist climate and have plenty of room to let these grow to their natural, towering heights. There are smaller, dwarf varieties (*keeping closer to six feet tall when mature*) that are fine for limited space gardens. In general, the dwarfs are more adaptable to cooler and drier conditions. Beware of growing bananas in windy conditions: the large leaves split and tatter easily.

PROTEAS

▢ Pincushion Protea (*Leucospermum cordifolium*)

▢ King Protea (*Protea cynaroides*)

Photo by Diane Sullivan.

The *Proteas* are showy shrubs that thrive in well-drained soil and full sun. Most are damaged under 28 degrees. These ornamental plants are native to the scrublands and woodlands in South Africa. Although they look exotic and tropical, *Proteas* do well in a warm Mediterranean-type climate with well-drained soil and even tolerate dry air. Some *Proteas* sport striking flowers that can look like bright colored curved pincushions (*like the Leucospermum cordifolium, which is technically not a Protea*) and others look as if the blossom were made out of colorful feathers. The King Protea (*Protea cynaroides*) is probably one of the best known species and makes a dramatic cut flower. Healthy shrubs usually grow from three to four feet tall, but can grow larger with some species reaching over twenty feet.

STRELITZIA NICOLAI

▢ Giant Bird of Paradise (*Strelitzia nicholia*)

Photo by Robert Bornstein.

The *Strelitzia nicolai*, or giant bird of paradise, is much like its cousin, the *Strelitzia reginea* (*bird of paradise*). It grows much taller — to a tree-like twenty or twenty-five feet — and has dark blue, almost black, and white, larger flowering versions of the blue and orange bird-like blooms seen in *Strelitzia reginea*. (*The smaller version is listed under 'Fabulous Flowers, Shrubs, and Vines'.*) Also a native of eastern South Africa, the giant bird of paradise needs the same care as its smaller relative. Both are evergreen. Give it sun or part shade, a rich humus type of soil, and a fair amount of water. It will be damaged in anything colder than a light frost.

ALPINIA

☐ Red and pink ginger (*Alpinia*)

Photo by Diane Sullivan.

Better known as ginger, the *Alpinia* is native to Southeast Asia where most species enjoy living in the rainforests. There are many varieties of ginger, some with colorful and decorative foliage. Others sport gaily painted flowers that almost look like they are works of art. One type of ginger, of course, is in major commercial production for its edible root. Alpinias tend to form clumps with their creeping rhizomatic roots. Give these plants sun, part sun, or shade, depending on the variety, and plenty of water. They will grow from two feet to eighteen feet tall. Most gingers for the garden average five to six feet. Growing gingers will certainly add a tropical flavor to the garden.

CANNA

☐ Canna lily (*Canna*)

The *Canna*, or the canna lily, in its wild form is native to the American tropics, but it has been inbred to produce large and colorful leaves and flowers that will thrive in temperate zones as well. The garden canna lily comes with large, showy leaves in dark reds or greens, patterned in designs, or splashed with streaks of colors including bright white, yellow, red, amber, mahogany, chartreuse, and almost-black. Flowers are showy, too, blooming in reds, oranges, yellows, whites, pinks, and are sometimes bicolor, spotted, or blotched. A versatile plant, this tuberous grower will spread to form colonies. It grows in soils that are soggy enough to sit in pond water or dry enough to be drought-resistant. Give it sun or shade. If your soil freezes hard in the winter, it is best to dig and store the roots in a cool, dark place. Plants can grow from two to nine feet tall.

ORNITHOGALUM

☐ Sun star (*Ornithogalum dubium*)

The *Ornithogalum* is a flowering plant that grows from a bulb. Most species and varieties are white flowering although there are some that sport rich orange or yellow flowers. The bulbs are indigenous to Eurasia and parts of Africa, and different kinds vary in their needs. The *Ornithogalum dubium*, the sun star or snake flower, is an orange variety from South Africa. It will grow to less than a foot tall even when in flower and does best without even a hint of frost. There are a number of white varieties that are more flexible in their garden needs and there is also a variety, the *Ornithogalum longibracteatum*, called the pregnant onion or the false sea onion, which will grow a couple of feet high. The pregnant onion sits with the bulb on the surface of the soil growing baby bulbs both on and all around it as new offset plantlets. It endures mild frost, sun, or shade, and a wide range of soils. This one is more of a curiosity. The *Ornithogalum* bulbs are not strictly tropical, but do add a tropical look to the garden.

SINNINGIA SPECIOSA

☐ Gloxinia (*Sinningia speciosa hybrid*)

The *Sinningia speciosa* hybrid, which you probably know as gloxinia, is a tuberous plant grown in warm gardens or as a houseplant. A true tropical grower from the rainforests of Brazil, it needs loose organic soil that stays moist. Give it shade and as much humidity as possible. A very showy plant, the gloxinia grows best with temperatures between 70 and 85 degrees.

Plant Character Profiles

ABOUTILON

- Flowering maple, Chinese lantern, or Chinese bellflower (*Aboutilon*)

The *Aboutilon* is another plant with an assortment of common names: flowering maple, Chinese lantern, and Chinese bellflower, among others. These charming plants with attractive maple-like leaves and decorative flowers need protection from heat, ocean salt, hot sun, and high winds. They prefer warmer climates and regular water. Most are indigenous to South America, though there are some exceptions, like the *Abutilon palmeri*, a native to the warm dry regions of Southern California. The better known garden plant, *Abutilon x hybridum*, is a frost tender shrub bred from species common to semitropical regions. Most of these grow to between three and nine feet in height. The flowering maple blooms in reds, oranges, yellows, pinks, whites, and soft pastel shades. Because of its maple shaped foliage, it can also be a good choice for a Japanese-themed garden. There are tropical and subtropical species native to all continents.

ACANTHUS MOLLIS

- Bear's breeches (*Acanthus mollis*)

The *Acanthus mollis*, or bear's breeches, is not truly from the tropics, but it sports big, wide foliage and tall spikes of white flowers often blushed with purple or pink that makes it appear tropical. It is native to southwestern Europe and the Mediterranean areas of the North African continent. It can take full sun in mild areas, but give it shade in hot sun. Somewhat drought-tolerant, the *Acanthus mollis* likes warm temperatures, average soil, and will tolerate some light frost since it usually goes deciduous (*dies back*) in the winter. Growing three to five feet high, the bear's breeches can grow wide with its one- to three-foot wide palmate leaves.

ANTHURIUM ANDRAENUM

- Flamingo lily or tail flower (*Anthurium andraeanum*)

The *Anthurium andraeanum* (*flamingo lily or tail flower*) is an eye-catching ornamental plant native to the warm tropical rainforests of Columbia and Ecuador. Flowering with brilliant red, white, coral, or pink waxy spathes that rise above broad, glossy, heart-shaped foliage, the flamingo lily is a glamorous addition to the warm, moist garden. It grows from twelve to eighteen inches high in soils with of plenty of well-drained, damp humus. In climates with low humidity or temperatures that drop below 50 to 60 degrees, it is best grown as a potted houseplant.

BAMBUSA VULGARIS 'VITTATA'

- Painted bamboo or Hawaiian golden bamboo (*Bambusa vulgaris 'Vittata'*)

Photo by Diane Sullivan.

The *Bambusa vulgaris 'Vittata'* (*Painted bamboo or Hawaiian golden bamboo*) is a very popular ornamental bamboo that can reach forty to fifty feet tall in wide clumps. With its colorful green-striped yellow culms (*stems*), it has been grown in warm climates for so long that no one is sure exactly where it originated. Many experts believe it likely evolved in Southeast Asia. Give this bamboo sun and plenty of moisture. Bamboos (*Bambusa*) are naturalized in Southeast Asia, Latin America, and some in Africa with a few scattered in other places around the world, including the United States. They can reach from one to over one hundred feet tall. Most can take sun and like plenty of water with heat and humidity, accepting winter temperatures down to the high twenties. Some, especially the ones that spread by runners rather than clumps, can be invasive and difficult to remove.

BERGENIA CORDIFOLIA

- Pigsqueak or heartleaf (*Bergenia cordifolia*)

The *Bergenia cordifolia* (*pigsqueak or heartleaf*) is a shade-loving Russian native plant that grows from ten to eighteen inches and blooms with clear pink flowers. Rambling over the soil surface, the pigsqueak covers itself with thick, rounded, or heart-shaped leaves that turn burgundy-bronze in the autumn. Needing little care, this plant gives the illusion of being tropical despite surviving chilly winters and requiring only ordinary soil and water. There are many hybrids with variable leaf shapes and autumn tints. Flower colors can be soft white, different shades of pink, deep red, or even purple.

CLERODENDRUM THOMSONIAE

☐ Bleeding heart vine (*Clerodendrum thomsoniae*)

Photo by Diane Sullivan.

The *Clerodendrum thomsoniae*, or bleeding heart vine, is a spectacular twining plant that can climb up to fifteen feet. It blooms with huge clusters of white lanterns with pure red central flowers set off against rich, dark green foliage. This plant developed naturally in tropical western Africa and won't be happy in temperatures under 45 degrees. It likes plenty of humidity and moist, but not wet, soil.

CODIAEUM VARIEGATUM

☐ Croton (*Codiaeum variegatum*)

The *Codiaeum variegatum*, or croton, is a popular garden plant in warm and humid climates. It is also a favorite houseplant. Native to open forests in southern Asia, Indonesia, and other Eastern Pacific islands, the wild form grows up to ten feet tall with mainly green foliage. There are numerous hybrids with brilliant foliage spotted, splotched, or tinted with yellow, red, pink, purple, white, orange, and green. Heights range between three and eight feet. Give them rich, moist soil with plenty of organic humus and grow them in bright, indirect sun or shade. Crotons are not at all frost tolerant.

CYCAS REVOLUTA

☐ Sago palm or sago cycad (*Cycas revoluta*) at the Japanese Garden at the Tillman Reclamation Plant, Van Nuys, California.

The Cycas revoluta (*sago palm or sago cyad*) grows as a native of southern Japan. It is not a palm at all, but like the Zamia (*see below*), it is a cyad: a member of an ancient plant family that was common during the Mesozoic period when the dinosaurs roamed the earth. It develops a broad trunk and grows with a crown of thickened compound leaves. The sago palm can be damaged from too much direct hot sun and temperatures much under 20 degrees. It needs warm summers and will do well with gentle sun or shade. Give it good drainage with ordinary or sandy garden soil. All parts of this plant are poisonous if eaten. Over time it will grow, very slowly, to twenty feet in height.

PACHYSTACHYS LUTEA

☐ Lollypop flower or golden shrimp plant (*Pachystachys lutea*)

Photo by Diane Sullivan.

The *Pachystachys lutea* (*lollypop flower or golden shrimp plant*) is only one of the colorful plants in the *Pachystachys* or *Justicia* group. Naturally growing in Central and South America, this heat-loving garden flower likes sun or part sun and regular garden soil. It will grow from two to four feet and can fill out to shrub-like proportions.

PHILODENDRON BIPINNATIFIDUM

☐ Selloum or lacy tree philodendron (*Philodendron selloum*)

Photo by Velvet Heller.

The *Philodendron bipinnatifidum* has a number of common names such as selloum, tree philodendron, split-leaf philodendron, and cut-leaf philodendron. It grows tree-like to about fifteen feet and often falls over with the weight of its huge leaves, continuing to snake along the ground. It can also grab onto tree trunks with its long, rope-like air roots and pull itself up to its full height. A shade-lover, this plant grows in the rich, moist soils of the rainforests in Paraguay, southeastern Brazil, parts of Argentina, and Bolivia. Warm climates can grow it in the outdoor garden with good soil and dappled or full shade. It also adapts well to pot culture for indoor planting.

PLUMERIA

☐ Frangipani (*Plumeria*)

The *Plumeria*, or frangipani, is a genus made up of flowering shrubs and trees that offer delightful perfumed blossoms, especially at night. Native to Central America, South America, and the Caribbean, Plumarias are not endemic to Hawaii even though most people associate them with the Islands. The fangipani need plenty of humidity, gentle sun or part shade, and coarse soil that will drain well. They don't like their feet staying wet. Tall varieties of plumaria can grow thirty or forty feet tall.

STRELITZIA REGINAE

◻ Bird of paradise (*Strelitzia reginae*)

The *Strelitzia reginae*, bird of paradise, was originally rooted in the lands of South Africa where it became accustomed to a moderate rainfall and a rich, slightly acid soil. It blooms best in full sun, but the foliage, large and thick, shows off best in shade, especially in drier climates. The plant grows with a clumping habit to a height of three to five feet. The blue and orange flowers grow in a bird-like form that leads to its common name (*also called crane flower*).

TACCA INTEGRIFOLIA

◻ White bat flower (*Tacca integrifolia*)

Photo by Diane Sullivan.

The *Tacca integrifolia*, or white bat flower, is a bizarre flower that will serve as a conversation piece. It is a true tropical plant native to South Africa, Australia, and Southeast Asia. There is also a black version of the Tacca, *Tacca chantrieri*. Both have wide flaring petals and very long whiskers that can dangle down a couple of feet. Unless you have genuinely tropical, shady, moist garden conditions, grow this exotic as a challenging indoor or greenhouse plant. Most plants grow from six inches to four feet in height. They make unique-looking attention-grabbers when in bloom.

ZAMIA

◻ Zamia (*Encephalartos ferox*) shows the cone (flower) of this male plant in the Zamia family. This *Encephalortos* variety is a very popularly grown cycad that does not like frost.

The *Zamia* is in the ancient family of Cyads (*like the Sago palm*) common to the Jurassic period in history. Zamias are indigenous from areas of Mexico, south to Bolivia, and east to the state of Georgia in the American continent. They are comfortable in the warm, humid conditions of tropical rainforests. The plant's thickened leaves form handsome heads of waxy, palm-like or fern-like foliage. They are often clump-forming over time. Highly ornamental, these tropical plants like conditions that are warm and moist with rich, organic soils. Over time they will grow taller with slowly developing trunks. Plan on these plants reaching little more than four feet tall in the average tropical garden.

COCOS NUCIFERA

▫ Coconut palm (*Cocos nucifera*) in a typical Florida landscape.

Photo by Robert Bornstein.

The *Cocos nucifera* is the familiar coconut palm romantically associated with the idealized tropical island paradise with its life-saving coconut fruit. It has been cultivated all over the world for so long in warm, humid climates that the exact point of origin is unknown, though it is believed to be somewhere in tropical Asia. To grow well, this tall palm needs toasty temperatures. Although it can survive an occasional bout with a light frost, these palms are happiest when temperatures remain between 65 and 85 degrees. They do well on sparse soils with excellent drainage in full sun. They are also very tolerant of salty, sandy soils near the ocean. The coconut palm will grow from eighty to one hundred feet in height. This is not the best palm for a small garden.

CARYOTA

▫ Fishtail palm (Caryota)

Photo by Velvet Heller.

The *Caryota*, or fishtail palm, offers over a dozen different species endemic to tropical, subtropical, and mountainous environments of the South Pacific and Asia. The fishtail palm grows between twenty to eighty feet tall depending on the species. These palms are frost sensitive. The ragged-ended leaves are decorative and the palm will grow well in good light indoors as a house plant. Outdoors give it rich soil and plenty of water with part shade.

PHOENIX ROEBELENII

▫ Miniature date palm or pigmy palm (*Phoenix roebelenii*)

The *Phoenix roebelenii* (*miniature date palm or pigmy palm*) is a handsome, low-growing palm that is easy to fit into Mediterranean or tropical-looking landscapes. Expect this small palm to grow from six to ten feet high and spread at least as wide. This palm is native to Southeast Asia, in particular Thailand and Burma (*currently called Myanmar*). Graceful with its long, arching fronds, it grows in sun to part shade. The pigmy palm also makes a good container plant. Quite drought-tolerant and accepting of various types of soils so long as they drain well, these palms should survive cold down to the low 20s, but will show browning damage with less frost.

CHAMAEROPS HUMILIS

▫ Mediterranean or European fan palm (*Chamaerops humilis*)

Photo by Diane Sullivan.

The *Chamaerops humilis* (*Mediterranean or European fan palm*) is a handsome, fan-leafed palm that makes its native home in the hot, dry slopes and mountains of the southwestern regions in the Mediterranean. Although these palms like it warm, the Mediterranean fan palm is one of the more cold-tolerant palm trees, withstanding temperatures as low as 10 degrees. Grow this palm in gardens with full sun and fast-draining soils that can be lean or rich. A drought-tolerant palm, foliage can vary from green tones that are bright to grey or even blush with a blue or yellow tint. This palm has a tendency to sucker, forming attractive clumps and keeping its height between five to twenty feet.

RHAPIS EXCELSA

▫ Broadleaf lady palm or bamboo palm (*Rhapis excelsa*)

The *Rhapis excelsa* (*broadleaf lady palm or bamboo palm*) is a fan palm that will grow from twelve to twenty feet tall. It is thought to be native to China or Taiwan, but it is no longer found in the wild: all specimens are cultivated. It will accept low light and low humidity as well as a wide range of soils. It will survive an occasional temperature dip into the 20s (*Fahrenheit*), but prefers winter temperatures to stay above freezing. The broadleaf lady palm isn't fussy about soil, is happy with regular water, and will grow in sun or shade, although the green of its ornamental leaves has a deeper color in shaded conditions.

SERENOA REPENS

▫ Saw palmetto (*Serenoa repens*)

Photo by Robert Bornstein.

The *Serenoa repens*, or saw palmetto, is a native that grows in the southeastern parts of the United States. This small palm is long-lived, slow-growing and tops out at between three to six feet in height. Clumps can be up to twenty feet in diameter. Leaves are variable in color from silver blue to lemony green. Although it is not frequently sold in garden centers outside the East Coast, it is a very versatile palm that can adapt well to seaside sand, damp forests, or dry scrubland gardens. Not fussy about light or soil, the saw palmetto is hardy to 10 degrees.

SYAGRUS ROMANZOFFIANA

▫ Queen palm
(*Syagrus romanzoffiana*)

The *Syagrus romanzoffiana* is the queen of palm trees. These trees have become very popular in Florida and California during the past decade. They make graceful trees when small and appear to fit nicely into small properties. They will, however, grow to 50 feet at maturity and if not planted wisely will end up looking like telephone poles in the small garden. Natural to South America in Argentina, Paraguay, Brazil, and Uruguay, the queen palm prefers a rich but sandy soil and plenty of sun.

These are the all-American plant performers at home in the wide area of grasslands, steppes, and prairies in the central part of the United States. Since this open area of the United States can experience very cold winters, most of these plants are very frost tolerant. Unless otherwise stated, expect that cold-hardiness is not a factor in growing the plains population plants profiled here.

PLAINS POPULATION

ANDROPOGON

- Bluestem (*Andropogon*)

Photo by R. Lutz.

The *Andropogon*, or bluestem, has many species and hybrids cultivated for garden use. A favorite is the *Andropogon 'Silver Sunrise'*, which is a cross between the Great Plains *Andropogon gerardii* and the sand bluestem, *Andropogon hallii (another native to the central plains of the United States)*. Although the foliage stays at about two feet tall, the flowering stalks can stretch up to five or six feet. This plant likes sun and free-draining, dry soils, but it is more adaptable than many other ornamental grasses when it comes to soil conditions. It is a very hardy ornamental grass.

DESCHAMPSIA CESPITOSA

- Tufted hairgrass or Tussock grass (*Deschampsia cespitosa*) shows off nicely in a stone landscape design.

Photo and plant design by Lisa Bourey.

The *Deschampsia cespitosa* (*tufted hairgrass or Tussock grass*) is an ornamental grass that grows naturally in the Americas and Eurasia in moist grasslands. At about two feet tall, it is a bunch grass with a delicate appearance that prefers cool growing conditions, but will accept heat so long as it has plenty of water. There are some very decorative cultivars and hybrids available for the garden. Give it full sun or part shade.

MUHLENBERGIA CAPILLARIS

- Pink muhly grass, pink hair grass, or hairawn muhly (*Muhlenbergia capillaris*)

The *Muhlenbergia capillaris* has a collection of common names like the pink muhly grass, pink hairgrass, or hairawn muhly. It is one of the few grasses that are colorful in bloom. The delicate pink inflorescences (*the stalk-like arrangement of tiny flowers typical in the true grass family*) look like pink or purple fairy dust and grace the garden in the autumn when little else is in bloom. They are particularly effective when the low rays of the sun shine through them and set them ablaze in bright pink-purple clouds. These are clump-forming grasses that range from one to three feet in height and about the same width. The pink muhly grass is most often found in sandy or well-drained woodland soils, coastal regions, or nestled into rocky areas. Growing well in moist or dry conditions, it grows naturally in the central and eastern parts of the United States and Mexico. It will often go dormant when temperatures go below about 15 degrees.

PANICUM VIRGATUM

- Switchgrass (*Panicum virgatum*)

Photo courtesy of GardenSoft.

The *Panicum virgatum*, or switchgrass, is one of the tall grasses of the prairies. It is a bunch grass that creeps along making thick stands of ornamental grass blades. This grass has suddenly grown in popularity as a crop cultivated for biofuel and for use in soil stabilization. It makes a handsome, cold and heat tolerant grass that grows three to six feet tall in full sun. It is also drought-resistant due to its deep and wide spreading roots. There are cultivars with colorful hues to the foliage or contrasting colored seed heads.

SCHIZYCHARIUM SCOPARIUM

- Little bluestem (*Schizycharium scoparium*)

Photo courtesy of Wildflower Farm.

The *Schizycharium scoparium*, or little bluestem, is a well-behaved, blue-tinted grass. It doesn't grow much taller than two feet in height and it will blush a handsome red in the autumn. This is another native to the Great Plains and has been adopted as Nebraska's state grass. Give it full sun, plenty of heat, and avoid being too generous with water if you want it to thrive in your garden. Little bluestem will also withstand extreme cold and wind. It may be small, but it's tough.

☐ Indian grass (*Sorghastrum nutans*)

Photo courtesy of Wildflower Farm.

The *Sorghastrum nutans*, or Indian grass, is a highly ornamental grass that is another native of the North American Great Plains. This is a warm-season grass that grows tall at three to seven feet and also likes to paint its foliage into shades of yellow or orange in the autumn. It will survive cold, frosty winters. Preferring a rich soil, Indian grass will tolerate anything from sand to clay. Although it is drought-resistant, it enjoys more water when it can get it. There are some very showy varieties like 'Bluebird', 'Sioux Blue', 'Indian Steele', and 'Holt'.

SPOROBOLUS HETEROLEPIS

☐ Prairie dropseed (*Sporobolus heterolepis*)

Photo courtesy of Wildflower Farm.

The *Sporobolus heterolepis*, or Prairie dropseed, is a decorative bunch grass with smooth, flat leaves that will look graceful in the garden. It's another autumn foliage show-stopper, clothing itself in a bright orange hue to celebrate the end of the growing season. This one is native from the East Coast through the Midwest of the United States. Prairie dropseed will grow two feet tall and a little less in width. Give it lots of sun and keep the soil on the dry side.

Flatland Ground-cover

Plains ground-covers offer colorful low-growers for open areas.

DALEA PURPUREA

□ *Purple prairie clover (Dalea purpurea)*

The *Dalea purpurea* is the purple prairie clover native to eastern and central United States. This decorative wildflower is perfect for sunny gardens with good drainage. The plants grow from one to three feet tall and can sprawl. Purple prairie clover is tolerant of both heat and cold, takes medium watering, and is an easy-care flowering plant for the garden.

AESCULUS PARVIFLORA

□ Bottlebrush buckeye (*Aesculus parviflora*)

Photo by Lisa Bourey.

The *Aesculus parviflora*, or bottlebrush buckeye, is a very hardy, large shrub to small tree of eight to twelve feet high and eight to fifteen feet wide. Butterflies and hummingbirds love to visit when it is in bloom. A handy-sized plant for shade or screening, the bottlebrush buckeye prefers an average to rich soil and partial or dappled sun. It is native to the open woodlands of Southeastern United States.

AMELANCHIER ALNIFOLIA

□ *Serviceberry breaking dormancy (Amelanchier)*

Photo by Kylee Baumle.

The *Amelanchier alnifolia*, or serviceberry, is another very cold-hardy plant. A highly adaptable shrub that is native to the northern, central, and western parts of North America, the serviceberry has decorative white flowers and edible red or dark/almost black fruit that attract birds. The serviceberry is at home from sea level right into the high mountains, accepting moist to dry soils and full sun to partial shade. Varieties of the Amelanchier can grow from three to thirty feet. There are a number of different serviceberry varieties that do well in temperate zones across the country. All have white flowers, decorative berries, and often put on blazing displays of colorful autumn foliage.

BERBERIS FENDLERI

□ *Fendler's barberry or the Colorado barberry (Berberis fendleri)*

Photo courtesy of Forestfarm.

The *Berberis fendleri* (*Fendler's barberry or the Colorado barborry*) is a deciduous (*loses its leaves in winter*) shrub that grows six to eight feet tall and equally wide. A home-grown, New Mexico, and Colorado native with yellow flowers and cheerful red berries, give this hardy plant rich soil, average water, and a bit of shade to encourage it to perform best. It is a good plant for a native garden in the Midwest and for slopes and canyons at higher elevations.

EUONYMUS ATROPURPUREA

□ *Eastern wahoo or burning bush (Euonymus atropurpurea)*

Photo courtesy of Easy Living Wildflowers.

The *Euonymus atropurpurea* (*Eastern wahoo or burning bush*) is a small tree or dense shrub that handles full sun to shade as well as cold winter temperatures. It offers small, handsome, reddish-pink fruits and the foliage turns a glowing red-orange autumn color. This ornamental plant evolved in the interior of the United States making its home on the open plains and into forested areas. Give this Euonynmus good drainage in the garden.

ALLIUM STELLATUM

□ Prairie onion or autumn onion
(*Allium stellatum*)

*Photo courtesy of Easy
Living Wildflowers.*

The *Allium stellatum* (*Prairie onion or autumn onion*) is a native onion that grows in the prairie areas of limestone rock in the Midwest. Flat grass-like leaves grow to about a foot tall and the flowers bloom with small, white, purple-pink, or red-pink bell-like blossoms. These bulbous plants grow in full sun with excellent drainage and have been used to help develop some more showy hybrids for garden culture as this wild onion crosses easily with other ornamental onion varieties. The prairie onion can be used to good effect in a wild, native garden design and is happy with cold winters and toasty summers.

LIATRIS PYCNOSTACHYA

□ *Prairie blazing star
(Liatris pycnostachya)*

*Photo courtesy of Easy
Living Wildflowers.*

The *Liatris pycnostachya*, or Prairie blazing star, is a bulbous plant that sends up tall pokers tipped with a spike of purple flowers. It will grow to four feet tall and is happy in full sun. Not fussy about soil or water, it will do well in damp or dry. There are a number of species, cultivars, and hybrids that range from purple through pink or white in color. They all do well with pretty much the same conditions, tolerating frost in the winter while dormant and enjoying plenty of heat in the summer.

ACHILLEA TOMENTOSA

☐ Woolly yarrow (*Achillea tomentosa*)

The *Achillea tomentosa*, or woolly yarrow, is a low grower that will stay under a foot in height, but spread widely, making it a good ground-cover. It is a natural resident of higher elevations and originally evolved in Europe, Eurasia, and Asia. There are many species of yarrow growing around the world, most preferring fast-draining soil and full sun, just like this one, although the woolly yarrow will tolerate some shade, too. Blooming with sunny yellow flowers, the woolly yarrow is ideal for cool climates and likes dry to average water.

AGASTACHE RUPESTRIS

☐ Red hyssop or licorice hyssop (*Agastache rupestris*)

Photo by Velvet Heller.

The *Agastache rupestris* (*red hyssop or licorice hyssop*) is a herb with fruity to minty scented leaves. It grows in good drainage with full sun. Native to mountainous slopes in the central to southwestern parts of the United States, it has other attractive and colorful cousins all over North America and in Asia. Growing with an upright habit, the red hyssop can reach three to four feet in height and will bloom with soft reddish flowers in cool or heat. There are many Agastache hybrids that offer a wide range of colors.

ASCLEPIAS TUBEROSA

☐ Butterfly weed (*Asclepias tuberosa*)

Photo by Velvet Heller.

The *Asclepias tuberosa* is a showy plant that has earned its common name: butterfly weed. It, like its fellow milkweeds, is one of the favorite foods of the Monarch butterfly caterpillars. The butterfly larvae will strip a plant leaving it skeletonized, yet the butterfly weed will grow back remarkably fast to bloom in brilliant red-orange flowers. Native to Eastern North America, plants can reach four feet tall and do best with well-drained soil of various compositions in full sun. For anyone who isn't a Monarch butterfly, all parts of the plant are poisonous when eaten. This *Asclepias* is also sometimes called pleurosy root.

BAPTISIA AUSTRALIS VAR. MINOR

☐ Blue indigo (*Baptisia australis*)

Photo by R. Lutz.

The *Baptisia australis var. minor* carries the common name of dwarf blue indigo. This is a smaller version of the blue false indigo, *Baptisia australis*, which grows to around five feet high. The dwarf version will stay under two feet. Both the large and the smaller *Baptisia* are natives from the mid-section of the United States spreading east and south to Texas. Both varieties are very pleased to bask in heat and full sun. Showy in flower and out, the *Baptisia australis* has medicinal uses as well as decorative value. Give it good-draining soil and keep children and pets from eating the seeds and pods that are poisonous.

CALLIRHOE INVOLUCRATA

☐ Poppy mallow or wine cup (*Callirhoe involucrata*)

Photo by Velvet Heller.

The *Callirhoe involucrata* (*poppy mallow or wine cup*) is a small but eye-catching plant with wine red or deep pink flowers. The poppy mallow is a lover of full sun and dry, fast-draining soils. This little plant handles dry air, hot temperatures, cool winters, and likes hills, rocky areas, and open woods. Growing six inches to a foot in height, it will sprawl to three feet, making it useful as a ground-cover plant or to cascade over walls and barriers. It loses its leaves in winter. Give it full sun or light shade with moist or dry soil. The poppy mallow is native to the central section of the United States, spilling into states both to the east and the west.

Plant Character Profiles

CALYLOPHUS SERRULATUS

- Prairie lode, yellow sundrop, or Great Plains primrose (*Calylophus serrulatus*)

Photo by Velvet Heller.

The *Calylophus serrulatus* (*prairie lode, yellow sundrop, or Great Plains primrose*) is another low-growing plant native to the dry areas of the Great Plains. It grows to about a foot and a half and becomes woody as it ages. There is at least one selection that stays at only six inches. The plants flower heavily in bright yellow in good drainage and full sun, and can handle cold winters. They will grow well in altitudes up to 7,000 feet.

CAMPSIS

- Trumpet vine or trumpet creeper (*Campsis tagliabuana 'Madam Galen'*)

The *Campsis*, or trumpet creeper, is an enthusiastic, red-flowered climber that can rampantly smother everything in its way. It blooms with showy red trumpet blooms. The *Campsis radicans* is an American native that does well in gardens throughout the Midwest as well as on both coasts. It likes full sun, a wide range of soils, and average water. The *Campsis x tagliabuana 'Madam Galen'* is a cross of the American and Chinese varieties and is a little less overwhelming. Both are good for attracting hummingbirds.

COREOPSIS LANCEOLATA

- Tickseed (*Coreopsis lanceolata*)

The *Coreopsis lanceolata* is commonly called tickseed because of the tick-like appearance of the seed. It is a yellow daisy-type flower that grows in dry soils in full sun. There are cultivars that range from dwarf plants of six inches to larger varieties like the giant tickseed that forms bouquets of daisies on plants up to three feet tall. Tickseed grows wild in dry areas like the West and the Plains. At home with a wide range of soils and tolerant of hot or cold weather, it is a very adaptable flower and should be easy to grow if given good drainage.

ECHINACEA PALLIDA

- Pale purple coneflower (*Echinacea pallida*)

Photo by Teresa Soule.

The *Echinacea pallida*, or pale purple coneflower, is happiest in full sun with excellent drainage. There are many different coneflowers, some of which will self-seed when content. The pale purple coneflower is very drought-tolerant and will grow tall and leggy if given too much water. Native to prairie and woodland areas of Eastern and Central North America, these coneflowers come in varieties that offer pink, purple, white, and yellow flowers with protruding central disks and drooping petals. To get the best performance from them, give them full sun and a soil that is not too rich. Other coneflower varieties grow from ten inches to a little over three feet. Like most of the Plains population, these coneflowers do fine in frosty winter cold or summer heat.

GAILLIARDIA PULCHELLA

- Blanket flower, Indian blanket, or firewheel (*Gailliardia pulchella*)

Photo by Velvet Heller.

The *Gailliardia pulchella* (*blanket flower, Indian blanket, or firewheel*) is a plant that will add lots of color with its prolific, bright red-orange-yellow, daisy-type flowers. These plants can be found along roadsides in the Southwest. Growing from one to two feet tall, they are not fussy about soil, love lots of sun, and, if happy, will willingly self-seed. They are daunted by neither hot nor cold temperatures.

GERANIUM SANGUINEUM

- Bloody crane's bill or crane's bill (*Geranium sanguineum*)

The *Geranium sanguineum* (*bloody crane's bill or just plain crane's bill*) gets its "bloody" common name from the magenta-red flowers and the blood-red foliage that the green leaves turn in the fall. The "crane's bill" refers to the shape of the seed pods. These are hardy, true geraniums that form handsome mounds of foliage. Native to Europe and Asia, the crane's bill thrives in a wide range of soils with regular water in sun or shade. This variety grows to a foot and a half in height and spreads at least half again as wide. Plants do better in some shade if temperatures get hot and they go dormant where winters are cold. They'll do well in the gardens of the prairies and plains.

The *Spiraea fritschiana* is called the Korean spirea or Fritsch's spirea. There are many different cultivars and hybrids of the Spirea; this one is well-adapted to the plains and the prairie environments. A well-shaped bush that turns yellow in the fall, the Korean spirea plant offers white or pink flowers and has a low habit of growth, staying to two or three feet. The Korean spirea is native to the rocky cliffs, slopes, and forest edges of China and Korea. It is very cold tolerant. Give it fast-draining soil and sun, part sun, or shade.

RUDBECKIA HIRTA

◻ Black-eyed Susan (*Rudbeckia hirta*)

The *Rudbeckia hirta*, or Black-eyed Susan, is a one- to two-foot tall North American native plant that blooms enthusiastically and has lent its genes to many cultivars and hybrids to produce single and double blooms in rusts, oranges, yellows, deep reds, dark browns, and some streaked or striped with combinations of these colors. Rudbeckias will die back in winter. They prefer full sun, soils that drain well, and they brave wind and cold, as well as summer heat.

SOLIDAGO

◻ Goldenrod (*Solidago*)

The *Solidago*, or goldenrod, is a dweller of open meadows. The native goldenrod will grow up to four feet tall. It likes lots of full sun and soil that drains well. Natural to pastures in the Americas and Eurasia, it will grow graceful arched sprays of tiny golden-yellow flowers in the informal garden. There are many cultivars and hybrids that give you choices for a wide range of gardening conditions. It has become invasive in some parts of China and Europe.

This is a sampling of coastline plants that are likely to enjoy good drainage. A number of these are drought-resistant plants that put up with sun, wind, and salt spray from the ocean. Beach babes will also grow further inland, happy in rocky areas or when keeping watch from the bluffs.

BEACH BABES

BOUGAINVILLEA

▫ Bougainvillea

The *Bougainvillea* is a garden favorite from South America. Some say it was originally found on the coast of Brazil. These are popular garden plants due to the colorful papery bracts that surround the small white flowers. The flamboyant Bougainvillea grows as a woody, twining vine that can ramble far and wide. It can cover walls, structures, or large fences. *Bougainvillea* plants range broadly in size — some as small as three feet, some that spread ten times that — with many hybrids mostly in pinks, purples, salmons, reds, and whites. The *bougainvillea* likes warm climates and most will stay evergreen if temperatures remain over 50 degrees and the plants remain reasonably well-watered. Quite drought-resistant, these plants will not tolerate constantly wet soil. They can handle only an occasional light frost without protection, especially when young. For coastal gardens, they offer a big splash of color. Be careful when planting the *Bougainvillea, though*: it doesn't like its roots disturbed.

AGAPANTHUS

▫ *African lily or lily of the Nile (Agapanthus)*

The *Agapanthus* (*African lily or lily of the Nile*) has bold, strap leaves with large globes of blue, purple, or white flowers. Natives of South Africa, they are accepting of variable soils so long as the soils drain well. They will also tolerate a very light frost. Give them full sun except in hot, inland areas where they will appreciate some shade. There are many cultivars with heights from about a foot to three feet. Some even have decorative yellow or white striped leaves.

CALLUNA VULGARIS

▫ *Heather (Calluna vulgaris)*

Photo by photo by GardenSoft.

The *Calluna vulgaris*, or heather, has many varieties and cultivars. This acid-loving plant will make a happy home on a beachfront property with vegetative soil, plenty of moisture, and either sun or a bit of shade. Not fond of extreme cold or heat, heather is perfect for those transition zones just back from the sandy or rocky beaches where the soil has more organic content. It comes from rural areas of Europe and Asia Minor where it often occupies moist spaces by the edge of pine or oak woodlands. Most of these colorful heathers bloom in reds, purples, pinks, and whites; they usually stay under two feet tall. There are some lovely hybrids available for the garden, but don't even try to grow the *Calluna* if you don't have acid soil!

ARMERIA MARITIMA SUBSP. CALIFORNICA

▫ California sea thrift, sea cushion, or sea pink (*Armeria maritima subsp. Californica*)

The *Armeria maritima subsp. californica* (*California sea thrift, sea cushion, or sea pink*) is a small, mound-forming plant that blooms with little, round, pink or purple flowers on straight, thin stalks that look like spherical lollypops. A sunshine lover, this little coastal native is natural to the West Coast of the United States. There are also a number of other *Ameria* species that hail from across the Northern Hemisphere and a few from South America. Not reliably frost tolerant, this little plant prefers light shade in hot-sun areas. It likes well-drained soil. The sea thrift can be used as a ground-cover or near the front of a garden border where its small stature and rounded tussocks of green foliage will look ornamental.

CEANOTHUS

□ Carmel Mountain Lilac (*Ceanothus griseus horizontalis 'Yankee Point'*)

The *Ceanothus*, or California lilac, has a native range from northeastern Canada to Guatemala with the largest concentration of species in California. There are low, ground-hugging shrubs of all sizes and several species that grow into small trees. Most are scented and bloom in tight clusters with blue, purple, lavender, pink, or white flowers. The majority of Ceanothus plants are evergreen. Many cultivars are available to fit just about any garden design. All like full sun to part shade, are drought-resistant, can handle light frost, and accept poor soils. One of the best for seaside planting is the wide-spreading *Ceanothus griseus horizontalis 'Yankee Point'* (the Carmel Mountain lilac) that will grow two to three feet tall, but easily spread ten feet wide.

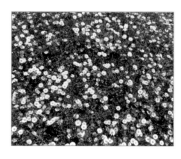

ERIGERON KARVINSKIANUS

□ Santa Barbara daisy, Mexican daisy, or fleabane (*Erigeron karvinskianus*)

The *Erigeron karvinskianus* (*Santa Barbara daisy, Mexican daisy, or fleabane*) originally came from South America and Mexico, but it has endeared itself to gardens all over the world with its sprawling little stems that are studded prolifically with little pinkish-white daisies. The Santa Barbara daisy has naturalized in many places to create new homes for itself where temperatures don't fall below 15 to 20 degrees. It can grow to three feet tall, but tends to spill over itself and spread to a wide mat of six inches to two feet tall. This daisy handles full sun or part shade and laughs at winds, salt air, and sandy soils. In fact, it is so adaptable it can sneak out of its garden boundaries and wander off on its own.

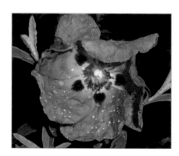

CISTUS PURPUREUS

□ Purple rockrose or orchid rockrose (*Cistus purpureus*)

The *Cistus purpureus* (*purple rockrose or orchid rockrose*) is not a rose at all, but grows into a rounded shrub that becomes smothered with white, pink, or lavender-pink open-faced flowers that do look somewhat like single roses. The rockrose is a tough plant that stays evergreen on its native dry or rocky soil and enjoys full sun. It originated in the Mediterranean, parts of the Middle East, and is also endemic to the Canary Islands. Growing from four to six feet tall and spreading a little wider, the *Cistus purpureus* is one of the coldest, salt and wind tolerant rockroses and grows well on sandy soils. It does well in temperatures above 15 degrees.

EUPATORIUM MACULATUM

□ Spotted Joe-Pye weed (*Eupatorium maculatum*)

The *Eupatorium maculatum* is known as the spotted Joe-Pye weed or sometimes just the Joe-Pye weed. It likes moist areas and full sun or part shade. A herbal plant that is native to the eastern parts of North America, it will grow from four to seven feet tall. Decorative lavender-pink flowers that are grouped to look like fluffy heads contrast well against the dark green foliage and offer a soft vanilla scent. The Joe-Pye weed is decorative with its deep green or purple flushed stems and foliage. It lends a woodland feel to the moister coastal garden. There are a number of cultivars and named hybrids with varied flower and leaf colors; most are quite frost hardy. The *Eupatorium maculatum* has recently been renamed *Eutrochium maculatum*.

CORREA 'IVORY BELLS'

□ *Correa 'Ivory Bells'*

The *Correa 'Ivory Bells'* is thought to be a hybrid from the Australian shrub, *Correa alba*. It is a handsome plant with decorative, off-white bell-like flowers. The three species most often grown (*or hybridized*) for the garden outside of Australia are the *Correa reflexa, Correa alba*, and *Correa pulchella*, although other varieties are also available and the different species often naturally cross-breed. Growing from prostrate up to twenty feet in their native habitat, most garden Correa plants range from one to four feet. The *Correa 'Ivory Bells'* like fast-draining soil and full sun to part shade. Being evergreen, it is ornamental both in and out of flower and will fill a four-foot space with nice, rounded growth. It will tolerate light frost, but like many Australian plants, it is shy of phosphorus in the soil.

FRAGARIA CHILOENSIS 'AULON'

□ Beach strawberry (*Fragaria chiloensis 'Aulon'*)

The *Fragaria chiloensis 'Aulon'* is rightfully known as the beach strawberry. It is indeed a true strawberry, but it is grown for its rich, green, tri-lobed foliage and relatively large white flowers. This low-growing ground-cover spreads wide, though the plant will likely not grow much taller than six inches. This is one of those plants that will do well in dry soils. The beach strawberry will enjoy fast-draining, sandy soils on the coast or inland and will appreciate a little protection from the hot sun. It will also tolerate the salt from ocean air. The beach strawberry is native to the western coastline up and down the American continent and is frost tender. It is edible, and the *Fragria chiloensis* is one of the plants that was used to develop the tasty strawberry grown commercially as well as in home gardens for consumption today.

from six inches to a foot and a half high. It likes full sun and is loved by birds and butterflies. Natively growing in shades of yellow, there are cultivars available in a wider range of colors for the garden. The common sun rose creates a small rounded ground-cover that smothers itself with brightly colored single five-petal, open-faced flowers. Give this plant fast-draining soil on the alkaline side. It likes sand and rock and can take temperatures well below freezing.

GREVILLEA

- Grevillea *'Watiki Sunrise'*
- Grevillea *Rosmarinifolia*
- Woolly Grevillea (Grevillea lanigera 'Prostrate')

Grevillea is a group of plants that range from creepers to trees. Many *Grevilleas* sport curious, colorful flowers with the bottle brush-like configuration that seems to be a characteristic notable in many Australian plants. Whether you grow the *Grevillea robusta* (*sometimes called the southern silky oak or silky-oak*) that can grow to ninety feet tall or the *Grevillea lanigera 'Prostrate Form'* (*Prostrate woolly grevillea*) that will stay under two feet high, give these plants fast-draining soil, preferably slightly on the acid side. Be cautious when feeding Grevilleas as they do not like

phosphorous. Some of the flowers are extremely showy and some of the leaves can also be decorative. Use these plants for character and color in dry, warm climates with full sun to light shade or try them out by the ocean where they will enjoy rocky or sandy soils and look great despite on-shore breezes. One of the best for the seaside garden is the *Grevillea lanigera*, the coastal gem Grevillea. Choose the variety or cultivar that fits best in your landscape design.

HELIANTHEMUM NUMMULARIUM

- *Common sun rose (Helianthemum nummularium)*

Photo by Velvet Heller.

The *Helianthemum nummularium* (*common sun rose*) is related to the rock rose. This cheerful plant is common throughout Europe and naturally grows

HELICTOTRICHON

- *Blue oat grass (Helictotrichon)*

The *Helictotrichon*, or blue oat grass, is an ornamental grass that evolved in the open grasslands of central Europe. It has a distinctive blue tint to the leaves that adds year-round color to the garden and can contrast artistically with other greens or darker foliage plants. It will tolerate temperatures that drop into the teens, but stays more attractive and evergreen with warmer temperatures. It accepts coastal conditions as well as inland heat. Not fussy about soils so long as they drain well, give the blue oat grass regular water and sun or part sun to grow it best. Plants usually grow from twelve to eighteen inches in height.

IRIS DOUGLASIANA

- *Douglas iris or Pacific Coast hybrid iris (Iris douglasiana)*

The *Iris douglasiana* (*Douglas iris or Pacific Coast hybrid iris*) is a native iris natural to the coastlines of California and Oregon. These are small irises from six to eighteen inches high. They form colonies of long, flat-bladed, evergreen foliage with flowers in a variety of shades mostly in blues, yellows, purples, and whites, but with some of the hybrids expanding into butterscotch and deep red tints. The flowers only last a day, but there is a regular succession of blooming in the clumps. Each flower can be painted with impressively decorative designs and some people think they look a lot like orchids. These irises grow in open woods, rocky slopes, or open fields near the ocean. They will appreciate well-drained soil in sun or shade and will survive mild frost.

JUNIPER HORIZONTALIS

- *Creeping juniper or creeping cedar (Juniper horizontalis) at the Hannah Carter Japanese Garden, Los Angeles, California.*

The *Juniper horizontalis* (*creeping juniper or creeping cedar*) naturally grows in rocky and gravelly conditions on North American slopes and shores. The plant grows four inches to two feet high and up to eight feet wide. There are many varieties with color variations that range through hues of green, yellow, white, and combinations of these colors. They are excellent ground-cover, useful for many design effects, and fine plants to use for erosion control. Both cold and heat tolerant, the creeping juniper is a good drought-tolerant plant for either full sun or light shade.

LANTANA

▫ *Lantana.*

Photo by Velvet Heller.

The *Lantana* comes in two habits of growth. The bush lantanas can grow up to six feet tall as a sprawling shrub while the trailing or weeping lantana, *Lantana montevidensis*, is a good ground-cover at six inches to a foot in height yet wide-spreading. Lantanas are from the tropical regions of the Americas and Africa. They will die back under 28 degrees and likely be killed with colder winter temperatures. Highly decorative and long blooming with their umbels (*clusters*) of red, yellow, white, purple, and pink flowers, lantanas take full sun or part shade. The *Lantana montevidensis* usually offers purple or white flowers whereas the bush varieties often show off multiple colors in each umbel. These plants like a wide variety of soils and are resistant to ocean salt spray. They have become serious invaders in places like Florida and parts of Australia, however.

LEONOTIS LEONURIS

▫ *Lion's tail or lion's ear (Leonotis leonuris)*

▫ *Lion's tail or lion's ear, mint (Leonotis menthifolia)*

The *Leonotis leonuris* (*lion's tail or lion's ear*) is commonly found in South Africa and parts of California and Australia. Flowers are usually orange and curved for pollinators like nectar-feeding birds and butterflies. Not reliably frost-hardy, the lion's tail likes fast-draining soils that are not too rich. It basks in full sun and will grow into a showy garden shrub of six to seven feet tall

on coasts and a little smaller inland with hot sun. There is a slightly smaller cultivar, the *Leonotis menthifolia*, which grows from two to three feet tall and has a softer-colored orange bloom.

MONARDA

▫ *Wild bergamot or beebalm (Monarda)*

Photo by Teresa Soule.

The *Monarda* is commonly called wild bergamot or beebalm. It is a decorative, flowering plant that grows from two to four feet tall and attracts hummingbirds and butterflies. Native to North America, this colorful plant likes well-drained but moist soil and plenty of sunshine; one species has risen to six feet tall. Beebalm is very cold hardy and there are cultivars and hybrids with showy flowers in an assortment of pinks, reds, purples, and whites. Happy in gardens from the prairies to the coasts, this plant makes a good landscape plant for beach gardens, too.

MYRICA CALIFORNICA

▫ *California Wax Myrtle, California Bayberry, or Pacific Wax Myrtle (Myrica californica), taken at the Castaic Water Agency — Conservatory Garden and Learning Center, Santa Clarita, California.*

The *Myrica californica* (*California Wax Myrtle, California Bayberry, or Pacific Wax Myrtle*) is a large shrub that is native to the Pacific Coast from Vancouver through Southern California. It grows six to fifteen feet tall reasonably fast and forms an excellent windbreak or hedge that can be particularly useful in exposed, windy, inland coastal, or beach gardens. It prefers cooler summer temperatures, accepts regular water, and is frost-hardy to about 20 degrees. It also takes pruning well.

NANDINA

▫ *Heavenly bamboo or sacred bamboo (Nandina)*

The *Nandina* (*heavenly bamboo or sacred bamboo*) is a popular garden plant that originated in Eastern Asia and India and has become another serious invader in Southeast United States. Because of its attractive bamboo-like stems, decorative red, orange, or pink flushed leaves, and ornamental panicles of white flowers that turn into cheerful orange berries, this is a favorite landscape plant for sun or shade. There are varieties and hybrids with different leaf forms that grow from one to six feet tall. Many offer a vertical effect in the landscape that is not common to a lot of garden plants. A true low-maintenance plant, the heavenly bamboo is not fussy about soil, sun, water, extreme summer heat, or cold down to 10 degrees, so it handles the challenges of coastal gardens easily.

PEROVSKIA ATRIPLICIFOLIA

- Russian sage
  (*Perovskia atriplicifolia*)

The *Perovskia atriplicifolia* is known by the name of Russian sage despite the fact it is neither Russian nor is it a sage. Instead it originates in the high desert areas of central Asia that include countries like Afghanistan, Pakistan, and Kazakhstan. It earned the title of sage because of the strong herbal scent of the foliage. The Russian sage is a handsome plant with delicate-looking whitish foliage and feathery lavender flowers. It is adaptable enough to take frost, heat, most soils, dry air, and wind. It likes good drainage so it will grow well in deserts, mountains, and regular well-drained gardens or coastlines. Because it tolerates salt spray and wind, it scores high points as a beach babe. Give it plenty of sun.

PHORMIUM

- *New Zealand flax*
  (*Phormium 'Jester'*)

The *Phormium*, or New Zealand flax, offers handsome sword-shaped foliage that adds a vertical element to the garden. New hybrids are coming to the market each year since these plants have proven excellent for providing colorful foliage effects for the landscape. New Zealand flax grows from a foot to eight feet or more in height. Foliage colors include an almost-black mahogany through bright pink, yellow, apricot, brick, red, russet, white, chartreuse, and blends, often patterned in stripes. Some cultivars can survive temperatures down to 20 degrees. Give them full sun in all but the hottest areas where they will benefit from some shade. These plants do come from New Zealand, the *Phormium cookianum* being found naturally growing from the coasts to the mountains as well as in the scrublands in between. The larger *Phormium tenax* tends to be more cold tolerant and is native to the wet marshes yet able to adapt to surprisingly dry conditions. Most of the cultivars and hybrids are both showier and more delicate than the native species.

PITTOSPORUM

- *The Japanese Pittosporum, Japanese mock-orange, or Japanese cheesewood (Pittosporum) taken at the Mildred E. Mathias Botanical Garden at UCLA, California.*

Photo by Velvet Heller.

The *Pittosporum* (*Japanese Pittosporum, Japanese mock-orange or Japanese cheesewood*) is originally from Japan, which you might have been able to guess by any of its common names. It is a popular landscape shrub due to its orange-blossom-scented clusters of white flowers and its flexible habits of growth and cultivation. It can be clipped into a formal hedge, grown into a small tree, or allowed to grow into a natural-looking small or large shrub. The *Japanese Pittosporum* is a good drought-resistant plant and will grow well with sun, shade, average soil, heat, and mild frosts. It makes a good windbreak plant for coastal landscapes. There are a number of named hybrids.

PULSATILLA VULGARIS

- Pasque flower
  (*Pulsatilla vulgaris*)

Photo by Lisa Bourey.

The *Pulsatilla vulgaris*, or pasque flower, is a unique-looking flower with blooms in lavender, white, deep red, pink, or blue. A small grower, the pasque flower usually grows under a foot and a half and blooms early in the season. Even the silky seed heads are ornamental. Natural to North America, Asia, and Europe, these flowers handle wind and cold, but need good drainage and soils on the dry side. In mild areas, the pasque flower revels in full sun. It will also grow well in partial shade.

ROSEMARINUS

- *Rosemary*
  (*Rosemarinus 'Ken Taylor'*)

The *Rosemarinus*, or rosemary, is a favorite for landscape design and herb gardens. Decorative and easy to grow in warm, dry climates, rosemary comes in low creeping varieties that make handsome ground-cover and cascading trailers. Other species and cultivars of rosemary can grow into neat or sprawling shrubs from two to six feet, often spreading wider than their height. This is a woody plant with concentrated oils that are good for cooking, cleaning, using for scents, and handmade crafts. The essential oils also make the plant flammable in wildfires. You can find varieties that flower in pale blue, lavender, pink, and bright blue. Most rosemary cultivars will tolerate winds and salt spray, so they are a good choice for coastal gardens that do not get heavy frost. Rosemary also grows well in dry, inland areas with full sun.

RUGOSA ROSEMARINUS

- *Japanese rose or the rugosa rose*
  (*Rugosa rosemarinus*)

Photo by Barbara Black.

The *Rugosa rosemarinus* (*Japanese rose or the rugosa rose*) is a charming shrub rose that blooms with open-faced, single flowers. It has been a favorite parent for breeding hybrid roses. Because of its ability to tolerate salt and wind, it is an excellent choice for beach plantings. Most commonly it grows in thickets and smothers itself with white or pink flowers. Since it evolved on the sand dunes of coastal, eastern Asia and northeast parts of China, Japan, and Korea, this natural rose is a top pick for coastal climates. It accepts full sun and is not fussy about soil so long as it drains well. These are easy-care, decorative roses that will re-bloom, survive frosty cold, and even make good hedges.

SANTOLINA

▢ Lavender cotton (*Santolina*)

The *Santolina*, or lavender cotton, looks like a small, neat shrub when young. It is a native of the Mediterranean area. Cultivars and hybrids can be found with foliage from chartreuse to gray-white and deep green. The blooms are button-like flowers in whites or yellows. Give the lavender cotton full sun and it will grow from six inches to two feet tall depending on the variety. Older plants can grow woody and rangy over time. It also takes well-drained soil and low to average water. This plant tolerates mild frost, winds, and high heat in coastal or inland gardens.

STIPA TENUISSIMA, NASSELLA TENUISSIMA

▢ Hair grass, Mexican needle grass, feathergrass or Texas tussock (*Stipa tenuissima or Nassella tenuissima*)

The Stipa tenuissima or Nassella tenuissima (Mexican hair grass or Texas tussock) is an ornamental grass that will grow happily on the sea coast or inland in warm locations. It is a fine, silky grass that grows like a ponytail of fine green hair to about a foot and a half and roughly a foot wide. It is graceful in the garden, but can self-seed prolifically where happy — to the point of becoming a pest. Grow it in a dry, sunny spot with excellent drainage. Native to southwestern North America and southern South America, it adds a delicate touch to the garden. Hair grass will do well in warm coastal to hot, dry, desert gardens with a little added irrigation.

VERBENA OFFICINALIS

▢ Common verbena or vervain (*Verbena officinalis*)

Photo by Jenny Peterson.

The *Verbena officinalis* (*common verbena or vervain*) is an European herb that has become a popular garden flower. The natural form has gentle purple-pink flowers and forms a frost-hardy plant about three feet tall. It has become naturalized in parts of North America. There are a number of different vervains available for the garden that offer purple, blue, pink, red, and white colored flowers in large and small sized plants. Two vervains from South America, the *Verbena rigida* and *Verbena bonariensis*, are showy, blue-purple flowered plants perfect for hot-sun and very dry conditions. There are seasonal annual Verbenas and longer-living perennials. Some are less frost-tolerant than others. Most show off well in coastal gardens.

Some of the general use plants I've categorized as "country cousins" have been bred for so many years that their country of origin is no longer clear. Some have species that are still widespread all over the world. Origin is less important since these garden plants do well in the majority of landscapes where conditions are controlled, soils can be amended, and protection can be offered when the weather becomes severe.

COUNTRY COUSINS

Plant Character Profiles

The Romantics
Here are some of the more traditional, Old World garden inhabitants.

ALCEA ROSEA

▫ Common hollyhock (*Alcea rosea*)

Photo by Teresa Soule.

The *Alcea rosea*, or common hollyhock, is a decorative, hardy, short-lived perennial or biennial (*a plant that grows the first year and then blooms and dies the second*). The hollyhock easily grows six to eight feet tall in full sun. It is a member of the large mallow family and is native to the Southwestern part of Asia or Asia Minor. Not fussy about soils, this plant will grow tall and narrow offering a vertical accent to the garden design. There are cultivars in almost every color with spires of single or double flowers topping each plant. Hollyhocks are easy to grow in cold or hot climates.

DELPHINIUM

▫ Larkspur (*Delphinium*)

The *Delphinium*, or Larkspur, has native species scattered all over temperate regions of the northern hemisphere, many in the United States, and some in the tropical mountains of northern Africa. This member of the buttercup family is found in alpine climates, meadows, woodlands, and even has species that have dry-adapted themselves to desert areas. Depending on where each species evolved, sizes can range from tiny to six-foot tall plants. *Delphinium* flowers are best known for their wide range of blue shades, but there are also plants that bloom in purple, white, pink, and yellow. There are native plants for most any garden soil in hot or cold climates, plus plenty of hybrids that offer growth habits and colors for just about any design.

HEMEROCALLIS

▫ Day lily (*Hemerocallis*)

The *Hemerocallis*, or day lily, is popular all over the world since there are varieties that are adaptable to gardens in most any climate. Thousands of species and hybrids offer a wide choice of flowers in warm tones of single colors, bi-colors, and patterned petals in multi-colors. Plants tend to grow between one and three feet tall and can form large clumps as their rhizomes spread. Some varieties of the day lily have edible flowers and some re-bloom for a longer season of flowering. It is hard to categorize the *Hemerocallis* since it is so adaptable, growing well in sun or shade, dry or normal soils, seaside gardens or higher elevations, and heat or cold. Since these plants are so versatile, I'm listing the day lily as one of the genial country cousins.

LONICERA X HECKROTTII 'GOLD FLAME'

- Gold Flame honeysuckle (*Lonicera x heckrottii 'Gold Flame'*)

The *Lonicera x heckrottii* 'Gold Flame' (*'Gold Flame' honeysuckle is sometimes spelled 'Goldflame'*) is a cross between the native American *Lonicera sempervirens* and the European native *Lonicera Americana*. (*It is interesting that the names of these plants are so misleading about their origins!*) The 'Gold Flame' is a well-behaved honeysuckle that will grow ten to fifteen feet in either full sun or part shade. Unlike the Japanese honeysuckle, *Lonicera japonica*, the 'Gold Flame' is not invasive. It grows lightly-scented pink, yellow, and white flowers as it twines up supports. Frost hardy and tolerant of high heat, this is an attractive and easily grown honeysuckle that takes medium to low water.

PAEONIA OFFICINALIS

- Common peony (*Paeonia officinalis*)

Photo by Teresa Soule.

The *Paeonia officinalis* (*common peony*) enjoys part sun and is native to Southern Europe, western North America, and Central Asia. It likes a rich loam that is neither very moist nor very dry. Peonies grow from eighteen inches to nine feet tall, but most garden plants average two to three feet. They prefer cool temperatures and don't flourish in hot, dry climates. One exception to this rule is the California peony (*Paeonia califonica*) that is dormant and demands dry soil during hot summers. There are many cultivars and hybrids of the common peony.

PRIMULA VULGARIS

- Common primrose (*Primula vulgaris*)

Photo by Teresa Soule.

The Primula vulgaris, or common primrose, is a familiar plant across its native home in southern Europe, northern Africa, and into Turkey and Iran. Growing from three inches to just under a foot, this little flower likes a rich garden soil with regular water. There are cultivars and hybrids that will produce little bouquets of flowers in just about any color you want. Grow them in part or full shade.

ROSA 'DAVID AUSTIN'

- David Austin rose (*Rosa 'David Austin'*).

Photo by Velvet Heller.

The *Rosa 'David Austin'*, or David Austin rose, is a large group of fragrant English roses bred for repeat blooming by rosarian David Austin. These are large scented roses that bloom with big, peony-like flowers that open in unfurling layers. They are often considered the epitome of the romantic, old fashioned, English rose. Give them the same care as other roses: deep watering, sun to part shade, soil with a little well-rotted manure dug in, regular feeding, and mulch. There are wide choices of colors and growth habits in the David Austin roses. Like most roses, they prefer cool over extreme heat. There are lovely native roses in Asia, North America, Europe, and Africa. These are the ancestors of today's garden roses. Roses have been bred for well over 2,000 years. Grow your local wild roses for their charm, plant the David Austin rose for a classic English rose effect, or check into many of the other lovely rose varieties available.

6

$\mathcal{Plant}$ $\mathcal{Character}$ $\mathcal{Profiles}$

The Workhorses or Supporting Roles

These plants are ideal for theme gardens, more recently popular with contemporary or environmental designs, or are simply versatile plants that fit into a wide cross-section of uses.

ARGYRANTHEMUM

◻ Marguerite daisy (*Argyranthemum*)

The *Argyranthemum*, or Marguerite daisy, is a well-behaved flowering plant that originated in the Canary Islands and Madeira. It is often mistaken for a chrysanthemum. Look for these plants to be smothered in brilliant pink, lemon yellow, apricot, or white daisy-type flowers when grown in full sun with well-drained, regular garden soil. They can be lightly drought-resistant and tend to grow into a neat mound. Although they will survive light frost, they are not long-lived perennials (*maybe two to five years*). Shearing flowers will keep them blooming longer, but they rarely need to be pruned to retain their mounded dome shape.

ILEX

◻ Holly (*Ilex*)

The *Ilex*, or holly, has over four hundred species across the world. Some are threatened with extinction. Most are cultivated for their colorful red berries. The *Ilex crenata* (*Japanese holly*) is one of the smaller evergreen holly shrubs. It grows six to ten feet in height and bears black berries whereas the *Ilex opaca* (*American holly*) will reach forty or fifty feet tall showing off red berries. Most holly varieties do best in cool climates with woodland conditions of rich, moist soil, but they also adapt to a wide range of climates. Popular for hedges and foundation planting, these evergreen shrubs often become the backbone of garden designs in cooler climates. There are many cultivars and hybrids. Prune them to keep them shapely and, depending on where they are grown, give them sun, part sun, or shade. Male plants need to be grown to pollinate the female plants if you want berries.

KNIPHOFIA

◻ Red hot poker, torch plant (*Kniphofia*)

The *Kniphofia* (*red hot poker or the torch plant*) naturally developed in southern and eastern Africa. Since the plant has proven to be very adaptable and adds character to the garden with its sculptural form and colorful flowers, there have been a lot of hybrid varieties produced. Sizes range from small dwarf plants to big dramatic torches. The *Kniphofia uvaria* is one of the most commonly planted cultivars offering flowers that start blooming in red, turn orange, and then yellow as they age...like a burning torch. The foliage grows one to two feet high, but the flower stems can stretch up to four feet tall or higher. The torch plant will handle high heat, dry air, and some frost.

LIGUSTRUM JAPONICUM

◻ Japanese privet (*Ligustrum japonicum*) at the Green Thumb Garden Center, Santa Clarita, California.

The *Ligustrum japonicum*, or Japanese privet, is a large shrub or tree that is usually seen at eight to ten feet tall, but can grow up to twenty feet. This is a commonly used plant for landscaping with its evergreen leaves and white flowers. It can be used for screening, hedges, or even grown in pots for a formal look. Trained on a single trunk it can be grown as a small tree. The privet is drought-resistant and will take full sun, part sun, or shade, accepting a wide range of soils. There are dwarf and variegated (*with white or yellow streaked leaves*) varieties available. Native to eastern Asia into Japan, the privet handles light frost and will be damaged if temperatures fall under the mid-20s. These plants can take severe or elaborate clipping, which is why privets are a favorite for topiary.

LUPINUS, LUPIN(E)

◻ Lupin(e) (*Lupinus*) garden hybrid.

The *Lupinus* or *Lupin(e)* is another group of showy flowering plants with a wide range in stature and habitat. The greatest concentrations tend to be in western and southern North America and Europe, although lupines are found all over the world. There are tiny lupines and even a

Mexican species that grows into a tree. Lupines grow in arctic regions, on mountain tops, in open fields, and, because they have the ability to fix nitrogen with their roots, can thrive on poor soils. In desert or chaparral areas, you can find some colorful lupines like the Arroyo Lupine (*Lupinus succulentus*). A beach beauty is the seashore lupine (*Lupinus littoralis*) while you can find the prairie lupine (*Lupinus lepidus*) growing happily on the open plains. Three lupines that grace the higher elevations of Alaska are the *Lupinus polyphyllus*, *Lupine articus*, and *Lupinus nootkatensis*. All lupins, whether spelled with the "e" or not, like fast-draining soils. There are hybrids that will look showy in most home gardens. There are probably native lupines to fit into any character role, which is why these versatile plants are listed with the easy-going country cousins.

STACHYS BYZANTINA, STACHYS LANATA

□ Lamb's ear (*Stachys byzantina, Stachys lanata*)

The *Stachys byzantina* or *Stachys lanata* gets its common name, lamb's ear, from its soft, fuzzy, long, oval leaves that are hard to resist patting. It is a native of Turkey, Iran, and Armenia, where it can endure very cold winters. Despite its soft, white-coated, delicate look, the Stachys is a tough ground-cover plant so long as you give it sun to partial shade, good drainage, and reasonably dry air. It does not do well in heat and high humidity. Expect it to grow leaves under ten inches tall and to reach up to a foot and a half when blooming with pink-purple, sometimes whitish, flowers.

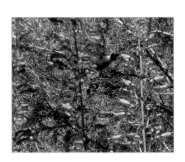

PENSTEMON

□ Beardtongue (*Penstemon spectabilis*) at the Theodore Payne Foundation for Wildflowers and Native Plants, Sun Valley, California.

The *Penstemon*, or Beardtongue, includes many decorative flowering plants in the roughly 270 species native to the North American continent and East Asia. There are low-growing, gritty *Penstemons* indigenous to the highest elevations, forest dwellers, natives of the prairie, and residents of the dry chaparral and deserts. Most like well-draining soils and plenty of sunshine. There are plenty of hybrids with showy flowers ideal for most gardens. There are so many choices in color and height that there should be a nice selection that will do well in just about anyone's garden.

RUELLIA BRITTONIANA

□ Mexican petunia (*Ruellia brittoniana*)

The *Ruellia brittoniana*, or Mexican petunia, grows about eight to twelve inches tall and will survive mild frost. The Mexican petunia is very showy when in full bloom with its silky purple flowers and dark violet stems. It is also a butterfly magnet. Although it likes regular water and good soil, it is highly adaptable and will spread into poor soils and thrive even in drought-tolerant gardens. Although the Mexican petunia is native to Mexico, it has invaded habitats in Florida, where it has become an undesirable pest; however, in some other areas, it can be a delightful garden flower.

SYMPHORICARPOS ALBUS

□ Snowberry, waxberry, or ghostberry (*Symphoricarpos albus*) with its tiny flowers.

Photo by Velvet Heller.

The *Symphoricarpos albus* (*snowberry, waxberry, or ghostberry*) prefers shady and moist areas with good drainage, but will tolerate some sun and can be somewhat drought-tolerant once established. Native to North America and Central America, with one species from China, the snowberry grows to about five feet tall and is planted not only for its attractive foliage, but for the showy, white, berry-like fruits it produces. A helpful wildlife food source in the native garden, this plant is perfect for creating thickets in an informal garden. It will take mild sun and is frost-hardy.

Plant Character Profiles

Some Familiar Bulbs and Corms

These are the heavily inbred bulbs that offer a wide selection of colors and forms seen in gardens all over the world.

HYACINTH

□ Hyacinth

Photo by Teresa Soule.

The *Hyacinth* is a bulbous plant native to Turkey, western Iran, and the eastern Mediterranean. These are popular bulbs that prefer some shade and light up the garden with colorful spikes of red, pink, blue, white, orange, yellow, lavender, and violet. Larger bulbs will grow into larger plants and over time will multiply to form colonies. The bulbs are poisonous. *Hyacinths* are usually delightfully scented and prefer cool climates over warm ones. Give them good garden soil and let the foliage die back after blooming to build up energy for next years' growth. *Hyacinths* can be dotted into the flower border, naturalized under trees, or massed for a powerful color impact. There are hybrids to offer color and texture to the flowering garden in different climates.

TULIPA GESNERIANA

□ *Didier's tulip or the gesnariad tulip (Tulipa gesneriana)*

Photo by Teresa Soule.

The *Tulipa gesneriana* (*Didier's tulip or the gesnariad tulip*) is the mother of most cultivated tulips used in popular landscapes. This bulbous plant is remarkably resistant to cold, though there are other species that are better adapted to heat. It is believed to have originally evolved in Asia. The gesnariad tulip and its hybrids will be happy with ordinary garden soil and sun or light shade. Just remember it will bloom for only a short time so be prepared to dig and save the bulbs after the foliage has died back or surround them with other plants to capture attention as tulip foliage begins to fade.

Herbal plants have been the primary source for medical care, crafts, and culinary arts for thousands of years. This is just a tiny sampling of all the wonderful herbs you can grow in the garden.

ARTEMISIA ABSINTHIUM

□ Wormwood, common wormwood, grand wormwood, sagebrush, or green ginger (*Artemisia absinthium*)

Photo by Genevieve Schmidt.

The *Artemisia absinthium* has a list of common names like wormwood, absinthium, absinthe wormwood, common wormwood, grand wormwood, sagebrush, and green ginger. It grows naturally in dry, rocky areas of Eurasia and northern parts of Africa. Wormwood has many herbal uses as a pesticide, flavoring, food coloring, and medicinal purposes. There are hundreds of species of *Artemesia* from all over the world; some being attractive with feathery whitish or green foliage and useful for their essential oils. Give them good drainage and lean to ordinary garden soil. Try *Artemisia* 'Powis Castle', *Artemisia versicolor* 'Seafoam', *Artemisia stelleriana* 'Silver Brocade', *Artemisia schmidtiana* 'Silver Mound', or *Artemisia ludoviciana* 'Valerie Finnis' for some of the best shapes, forms, and colors. Most will take at least some frost. These are adaptable to garden conditions in deserts, plains, mountains, and seashores.

ALCHEMILLA MOLLIS

□ Lady's mantle (*Alchemilla mollis*)

The *Alchemilla mollis*, or Lady's mantle, is a herb that makes a handsome ground-cover with its rich green, rounded leaves and bright chartreuse flowers (*devoid of petals*) lifted above the foliage in frothy panicles. The Lady's mantle grows in neat mounds from twelve to eighteen inches high. This is a native of southern and southeastern Europe grown for its ornamental, lush foliage or for its unique properties of collecting silvery beads of water on the flat, open leaves. This is not one of the species that is used medicinally. Give it mild sun or some shade and ample water. The Lady's mantle is very cold tolerant.

ASPERULA ODORATA

□ *Sweet woodruff (Asperula odorata)*

Photo by Kylee Baumle.

The *Asperula odorata* is a low-growing herb known as sweet woodruff. It will form a clump of foliage from six to fifteen inches high and flowers in white. Sweet woodruff makes a good ground-cover in shade and does best with moisture-retaining humus. Grown for its scent, as a flavoring, and for its medicinal properties, this herb is useful to add a lush feel to a landscape. It is native to Europe, western Asia, and parts of northern Africa. Sweet Woodruff likes frosty temperatures in winter.

ALLIUM SCHOENOPRASUM

□ Chive (*Allium schoenoprasum*)

Photo by Velvet Heller.

The *Allium schoenoprasum*, or chive, is the smallest member of the edible onion family. Naturally growing in North America, Asia, and Europe, these little onion bulbs form tight clumps and send up long, thin, hollow leaves that are often used fresh or in cooking. Flowers are decorative in pink-purple spheres of tiny flowers. Chives grow well in regular garden soil with average water in full sun to part shade. They are not very fussy about their water and soil demands. They die back to the bulbs in winter and can sleep safely through cold winters.

NEPETA

☐ Catmint or catnip (*Nepeta*)

Photo by Velvet Heller.

The Nepeta, famous as catnip or catmint, is a group of mounding plants that are in the mint family. They get their names from the olfactory stimulation experienced by many cats. They also offer nicely scented plants with decorative lilac, white, blue, pink, or purple flowers for the garden. Natives of Asia, Africa, and Europe, the catmints can take regular garden conditions or hot, sunny exposures where drought-resistant plants are needed. Most garden varieties die back in the winter and can take very cold temperatures so long as their feet don't stay wet. Give them sun or shade and minimal care, but don't forget to pinch off a few leaves if your cat has inherited the gene to enjoy a sniff, a rub, and a roll. *Nepeta cataria* (*catnip*) is the favorite *Nepeta* choice of indulgent felines.

ORIGANUM VULGARE 'AUREUM'

☐ *Golden oregano 'Aureum'*
   (Origanum vulgare)

The *Origanum vulgare 'Aureum'*, or golden oregano, is native to the western and southwestern parts of Eurasia and much of the Mediterranean. This is a low-growing, mat-like, ground-cover plant that stays between six inches and a foot in height. It takes full sun to partial shade and is perfectly happy in sandy or rocky soils. Not only is the chartreuse hue to the small leaves highly decorative in the garden, but the plant is edible and just as tasty as the common oregano. In fact, you can get a nice effect by planting the green and gold varieties side-by-side. Frost sensitive, grow the golden oregano as an annual in cold winter areas.

SALVIA OFFICINALI

☐ Culinary sage (*Salvia officinalis*)

Salvia officinalis is the Latin name for culinary sage. Growing a bit over three feet high, this plant likes ordinary water and prefers full sun. It has decorative spikes of blue flowers. There are hybrids with very colorful leaves like the *Salvia officinalis* 'Icterina'; 'Golden Garden Sage', Salvia 'Tricolor', and *Salvia officinalis* 'Purpurea' that are good in the kitchen, too. Give culinary sage protection in frosty winters. These plants are native to the warmer parts of the Mediterranean and need a soil with good drainage that isn't too rich.

THYMUS VULGARIS

☐ Common thyme (*Thymus vulgaris*)

Thymus vulgaris is the common thyme native to the Mediterranean and used in gardens worldwide for décor, cooking, and medicinal qualities. A small-growing, woody herb, this tiny-leafed plant grows from six to eight inches tall. Thyme species offer cultivars and hybrids with leaves that are fuzzy, colorful, or highly scented. They light up with pink, lavender, purple, or white flowers when in bloom. Excellent ground-cover and fillers for small gaps in the garden, thyme takes sun or part shade, many types of well-drained soil, and can handle some frost if the soil is not too wet.

Enough reading and applause for your performing plants. It's time to get your hands dirty.
Go have fun in the garden and create a fabulous garden show of your own!

Index